KOSHER CHINESE

KOSHER CHINESE

Living, Teaching,

and Eating

with China's

Other Billion

Michael Levy

A Holt Paperback
Henry Holt and Company
New York

Henry Holt and Company, LLC
Publishers since 1866
175 Fifth Avenue
New York, New York 10010
www.henryholt.com

Henry Holt® and 🏛® are registered trademarks of Henry Holt and Company, LLC.

Library of Congress Cataloging-in-Publication Data

Levy, Michael.
    Kosher Chinese : living, teaching, and eating with China's other billion / Michael
Levy.
        p.   cm.
    "A Holt Paperback."
    ISBN 978-0-8050-9196-0
    1. Levy, Michael. 2. China—Description and travel. 3. China—Social life
and customs—2002– 4. Jews, American—China—Biography. 5. Americans—
Travel—China—Biography. 6. Volunteer workers in social service—China—
Biography. 7. Peace Corps (U.S.)—Biography. I. title.
    DS712.L48 2011
    305.892'4051092—dc22
    [B]
                                                                                                                2010040319

Henry Holt books are available for special promotions and premiums.
For details contact: Director, Special Markets.

First Edition 2011

Designed by Meryl Sussman Levavi

Printed in the United States of America

10 9 8 7 6 5 4 3 2 1

Disclaimer: The material in this book comes from the memory and notes of the author.
All mistakes are his own. Where subject matter is sensitive, some characters' names
and identifying features have been changed. China is not as repressive as it once was,
but the author doesn't want any of his old friends getting into trouble.

for PCVs and RPCVs worldwide

入乡随俗

Contents

KOSHER CHINESE

Preface
The People Who Are Special, Too

I strongly believe there is no species of millipede I will ever find palatable. The particular version I found in my bowl on a warm summer evening in the summer of 2005 was an easy call. There were hundreds of them, red and pink, each about an inch long. They had however many legs it takes to make something "milli" as well as angry-looking pincers from both the front and back. They had been deep fried and were left moist with oil. The dish included long sugar sticks that one could lick and dip into the bowl. The millipedes that stuck would get sucked off the stick in what I had been assured was a delicious combination of sweet and sour. Nevertheless, I demurred.

"I cannot eat this," I told my host, a middle-aged Communist Party official in a dusty blue jacket. We were two of the dozen or so people who had gathered at the center of Unicorn Hill Village #3—a tiny hamlet of perhaps thirty single-story houses constructed of cinder block and wood—to celebrate my visit and the arrival of the Peace Corps. We were sitting around a low, round table on fourteen-inch-high plastic stools. The millipedes glistened before me in a chipped porcelain bowl. The group stared on in silence as the village leader looked from me to the millipedes and back to me. He had a spindly frame and tanned skin that was drawn taut against his cheekbones. He looked like a Chinese Voldemort.

"Eat the food," he grunted. His wife had made the millipede dish according to what my guide told me was "a very special recipe of the Bouyei people." The Bouyei were a tiny, impoverished ethnic group concentrated in the mountains of central China. These were some of the very people the Peace Corps had sent me to live with, learn from, and—in theory—teach. My first meal in the village and I was off to a bad start.

"You *can* eat this," my guide said with a nervous smile. "It tastes good." He demonstrated for me, licking his sugar stick, dipping it in the bowl, and sucking off one particularly hairy millipede. "They're sweet," he explained, crunching away happily, "and Americans like sweet things."

I nodded. "That's true." I groped for a polite escape. "But I'm a little different than most Americans." This gained me perplexed looks from both my guide and my host.

"I'm a Jew."

Gasps. Widened eyes. Furrowed brows. Awkward silence. I said this last sentence in Chinese. "*Wo shi youtairen.*" The phrase, loosely translated, meant "I Am a Person Who Is Special, Too."

Why—oh why—had I said this? This was atheist, Communist China, after all. Didn't Karl Marx say religion was the "opiate of the masses"? Had I just told my hosts I was a drug addict? And hadn't Chairman Mao condemned religion as one of the "Four Olds," a remnant (along with old culture, old habits, and old ideas) of the feudal past the Communist Party sought to destroy? I wondered if the arrest and deportation of a Peace Corps volunteer would make the evening news back home in Philadelphia.

As the silence around the table deepened and my face turned ever-darker shades of red, I marveled at the desperation of my religious *mea culpa*. I should have known better. I had, after all, already undergone months of Peace Corps training, sweating through seemingly endless hours of language classes, daily safety-and-security lectures, and occasional lessons in cross-cultural sensitivity. All of this, however, had taken place in Chengdu, the wealthy, relatively Americanized capital city of Sichuan Province, which was now a sixteen-hour train ride to the north. Chengdu had McDonald's, Starbucks, and an IKEA. It was the China of Thomas Friedman and other American pundits touting China's rise. I was now in Guizhou Province, the desperately poor, rural province in the dead center of China that would be my home for the next two years. Guizhou had . . . millipedes.

I was happy that my training was complete and I was finally on my own. I was happy to be in a part of China I had rarely seen covered in the American media. I was feeling like an authentic, trailblazing Peace Corps volunteer on an Indiana Jones adventure. Unicorn Hill Village #3 was no Temple of Doom, but this was far from my typical dinner.

Dr. Jones played it cool; I was desperate. Embracing my Jewish roots at that particular moment was a foggy-headed attempt to get excused from the table. I had never yearned so powerfully for a bagel.

"Jews can't eat insects," I mumbled, my eyes scanning for reactions from the men who surrounded me. "I don't want to get into it, but there are a lot of rules for us . . ."

The tension seemed to mount until, quite suddenly, the silence was broken by a hoot from my host's wife. Her cry was followed by smiles from others in the group, pats on my back, and even some applause.

"Comrade Marx was Jewish," said a man sitting a few paces away from the table, staring at me intensely.

"So was Einstein," beamed the man to my right, offering me a cigarette.

"You must be very clever," said my guide, as the bowl of

insects was removed from my side of the table, replaced by a dish of steaming meat.

"Why would the CIA send us a Jew?" mumbled Voldemort. I wasn't sure I had heard him correctly, but the raised eyebrow from my guide let me know I had, officially, just been accused of being a spy.

It was all a little bewildering, but I smiled like an idiot, happy to avoid the millipedes. I dug right into the mystery meat, and the men around the table quickly began eating their food as well. There was a toast to my health, then another to my success as a teacher, then another to American-Chinese friendship. We all got good and drunk.

I had passed the test. I was a Jew in the middle of nowhere, China.

Take Me Home,
Country Roads

Jian Nan Chun airlines flight 100, direct from Beijing to Chengdu, offered me my first glimpse into life in a country of more than a billion people. I walked to my seat midway down the aisle and settled in next to an old Chinese lady with thinning gray hair. She was munching on spicy chicken feet and silently offered me a bite. I politely declined. She belched in response.

Together, we watched the rows fill in front of us. We also watched as a handful of passengers struggled to find their seats. They looked from their boarding passes to the numbers above the seats, and back to their boarding passes. Eventually, though all the seats were taken, four people stood in the aisle moving in confused circles. The flight, it seemed, was standing-room only. I sighed, feeling pity for the four passengers who would now be delayed. "What a bummer," I mumbled.

Yes and no. A stewardess guided the four standing passengers towards the back of the plane where they doubled up with others. There was a bit of grumbling, especially from a petite octogenarian who ended up with a chubby teenager on his lap, but the eight people crammed into four small seats quickly struck up conversations with each other and began sharing cigarettes. We prepared for liftoff.

Lesson one from China: *overpopulation leads to a certain flexibility when it comes to definitions of both comfort and safety.*

I was one of fifty-seven Peace Corps trainees sprinkled throughout the plane. We were giddy, apprehensive, and fidgety as we imagined the ten weeks of training awaiting us in western China. It was meant to be an all-encompassing immersion that would prepare us for two years of volunteer teaching. We knew we would learn Chinese. Beyond this, however, we had only vague notions of what was to come.

The televisions in the cabin blinked to life and the steward-ess who had solved the seating problem popped what appeared to be a Betamax cassette into a machine hidden in an over-head compartment. An Asian man in a white lab coat appeared in grainy Technicolor. I felt for a moment like I was watching an instructional video from the Dharma Initiative.

The video was in Mandarin with Japanese subtitles, so I wasn't entirely sure what was being communicated, but the tenor of the video—and the images of people panicking during a simu-lated emergency landing—led me to believe that an English translation of the voice-over would have included the following fortune-cookie wisdom: "In case of emergency, accept your fate." The actors in the video pantomimed the crash-landing pro-tocol for passengers: we were to remove our shoes and cover our eyes.

As the plane took flight, exhaustion from the first two legs of my trip—from Philadelphia to San Francisco and San Francisco to Beijing—hit me hard. I fell into a fitful sleep. I dreamed of rice paddies and kung fu, egg rolls and Chairman Mao. I dreamed of my childhood fantasy of digging a tunnel to China. I dreamed of Phil, the Chinese guy who lived next to me during my fresh-man year of college. He was five feet tall, rarely left his room, and seemed terrified of me and everyone else on our floor. He even bought a Door Club to protect himself (protection from whom? We lived in a section of Ithaca, New York, where the worst crimes were teen drinking and public nudity). Phil almost drowned on his first day at school during the mandatory swim test. The lifeguard had to fish him out of the deep end of the pool with one of those giant metal hooks. "I cramped," he later explained.

Phil dropped out after a year of overly intense studying. If I survived the ten weeks of training and actually made it to my official site, would I find myself teaching hundreds of Phils? Would I have roomfuls of robotic students who could memorize instantly but were barely functional as social beings? Would stereotypes of Chinese students hold true? My nap was full of questions.

An hour later, I awoke to find the plane beginning a slow descent into a brown soup of pollution. We had almost arrived in Chengdu, the massive capital city of Sichuan Province and the home of the Peace Corps headquarters in China. The city was part of China's economic miracle and its corresponding industrial nightmare. Twelve million residents operated in an unregulated, crony-capitalist dream, generating a thick, pore-clogging smog. "It's like Luke Skywalker landing on Dagobah," I said to the old woman next to me. She smiled and spit out a chicken talon.

When I exited the plane, I was knocked dizzy by the evening heat. I imagined the capillary veins in my lungs recoiling in horror as breath after constricted breath dumped carcinogenic particulate matter into my previously healthy chest cavity. It wouldn't be long before my Chinese teacher would tell me that smoking cigarettes was actually healthy because it prepared one's lungs for Chinese air. The tobacco, she insisted, served as a vaccine against the smog. This seemed far-fetched to me, though I reconsidered my convictions after the Peace Corps nurse advised us to cease all exercise. An increased heart rate, she warned us, would lead to deeper breathing which, in Chengdu, meant a more profoundly damaged cardiovascular system. Best to sit and smoke, perhaps.

I shimmied down the movable staircase that had been wheeled over and gathered with the other trainees in a muted huddle. Before departing from San Francisco, there had been fifty-eight of us, but one trainee dropped out before even boarding the plane. As time passed, we knew our numbers would continue to dwindle; the Peace Corps typically loses a handful of people during training and a lot more during the remaining two years of service. Worldwide averages told us that by the end of our twenty-seven-month assignment, 30 percent of our group would already be home. In the parlance of the organization, these folks would suffer from "Early Termination," a phrase that made me think of Arnold Schwarzenegger. Who in this group would be Terminated? Who would make like Sarah Connor and survive? I looked at people out of the corners of my eyes. The tall sorority girl? The barrel-chested guy in the suit? I had the feeling people were giving me the same once-over. I tried to put a look of determination on my face but worried it just made me look like I had to use the bathroom (which, in fact, I did). I switched to a look that attempted nonchalance. I caught my reflection in an airport window and realized I merely looked slack-jawed and confused.

I knew I wasn't the only one who was worried and self-conscious, but this feeling of solidarity did not help allay my concerns. Western China, we all knew, would not be an easy place for most of us to live. It was beyond our frame of reference. We had all read Nicholas Kristoff's heartrending accounts of brutal Community Party repression, Fareed Zakaria's predictions about the future of U.S.-Chinese relations, and books swooning about China's economy with titles like *China Rises* or *The Chinese Century*. None of this helped me feel any confidence, however, since none of it had to do with actual daily life on China's streets. What was Chinese food like when actually eaten in China? How would I do laundry? What did ordinary Chinese think about Americans? What time would I go to sleep at night, and what time would I wake up in the morning? No question was too mundane, and as I stood on the runway in Chengdu with my fellow trainees, all of the pundits faded away. I felt the sun burning my skin, the smog filling my lungs, and the sounds of the teeming crowds in the airport. My senses were overloaded as the reality of the situation settled over me. I felt like Neo waking up in the goo of the Matrix reality.

◇

We soon arrived at baggage claim. As I waited for my backpack, a thought occurred to me. Or if not a thought then a feeling, or perhaps a revelation. It was this: "Within the next two minutes I will use a squat toilet for the first time in my life." I made my way towards the men's room.

I was excited. I had never used a squat toilet before and I was curious about the technology. The whole idea was new to me. I had, in fact, been surprised and amused when I first heard a toilet described as "Western." Movies, I knew, could be Western, as could saddles. But toilets? I imagined urinals that shined boots, or leather toilets with stirrups. How much diversity could there really be in the world of the toilet? What were the differences between the "Western" and "squat" varieties? These were some of the questions about life in China the New York Times had never answered.

Only one thing was certain as I approached the bathroom, and it was my extreme inflexibility. My "squat" was more like a hip bend with a slight lean. This, I knew, would create all sorts of problems, though I wasn't too clear on the geometry of a successful delivery. The shortest distance between two points is a line. I remembered that from high school. It seemed somehow relevant.

I entered the bathroom and waited my turn. My bowel discomfort grew in inverse proportion to the number of people in line in front of me. There were six Chinese men waiting for a stall. Each was wearing shiny black-leather shoes and a sports coat over a T-shirt. All six were smoking. They all had man-purses tucked under their arms. One of them was humming the John Denver song, "Take Me Home, Country Roads." The six-man line was reduced to five.

I was surprised by how badly my stomach felt. The food we had eaten since landing in China twenty-four hours earlier had been greasy and spicy, but I always thought of myself as fairly impervious to indigestion. I started singing along with the humming to distract myself.

Take me home, country roads to the place I belong

The other men in line looked over their shoulders at me. Then, without warning, they all joined me for the next line of the song:

West Virginia, mountain mama, take me home,
country roads

How could all of these men know the lyrics to this song? Was it possible that they would celebrate the entire John Denver collection? I would soon learn that Michael Bolton, Céline Dion, and the Carpenters were equally popular in China, but at that moment I was clenching my bowels far too tightly to think deeply on the soft power of American easy listening.

Two men now stood between me and my dream. My intestines churned and I fell silent. The man in front of me started up with the next verse of the song, turning to look at me when I did not join him. He saw the expression on my face, nodded at me with knowing concern, and cut his singing short.

Finally, blessedly, I was next. I rushed ahead. The stall was reasonably clean and I was pleased to find a sturdy lock on the door. I shut myself in and turned to face the toilet. But it was missing. In its place was a mere hole in the ground, surrounded by porcelain. The porcelain was a nice gesture but it did not distract me from the sickening realization that there was, in fact, no such thing as a "squat toilet." The phrase had apparently been invented to put real toilet users at ease. A toilet is a toilet, and a hole is a hole. I was standing over a hole. I felt cheated.

Regardless of the nomenclature, I was confronted with a vexing dilemma: which direction was I supposed to face? It wasn't clear to me how I ought to position my feet. Should they point towards the door, as they did while sitting in stalls in America? Or should I reverse direction in homage to being on the other side of the globe? I decided to face the wall.

I also wasn't sure if I was supposed to keep my pants on or remove them entirely. With pants on, I didn't see how I could prevent them from touching the ground as I squatted. The stall was clean, but the floor was definitely off-limits to anything other than the bottoms of my shoes. I grew up with a typically fastidious Jewish grandmother, and I inherited her distaste for disorder. She would follow family members around and clean anything they touched. She would refold my grandfather's newspaper each time he put it down; she would trail my father with a broom as he gardened, sweeping away any dirt that fell onto the driveway; she would wash each item of my clothing as soon as I took it off. I'm no Jewish grandmother, but I am infected with the same fear of the unclean.

I decided to remove my pants. I took off my left shoe and pant leg, lay toilet paper on the floor in a little sanitary island, and stepped on top. I repeated the procedure with my right shoe and leg and managed to get my pants off without stepping on the floor. All the while I was groaning and clenching my sphincter muscles. I tucked my pants under my armpit and moved into my best squat, a creaking version of the real deal. I teetered dangerously above the hole in the ground, thighs and calves burning. My hips soon threatened to lock and I bailed out, returning to standing position. I was mortified by my failure and moving towards white-hot panic. Luckily, there was a water pipe jutting out of the wall. I grabbed it and leaned backwards, now well positioned for the business at hand. As I relaxed, I felt my first, tiny victory over the challenges of life in China. I had also learned my second lesson: *only enter stalls with handholds.*

◇

We soon left the airport and boarded a bus heading for the center of Chengdu. As we zipped down a newly constructed, nearly empty highway, I reflected on what I knew about China and its people. I knew there were tens of millions of Chinese enjoying an economic boom in cities like Shanghai and Hong Kong in the south. There were tens of millions more committed to China's traditions—both Imperial and Communist—in Beijing to the east. Still others suffered, far to the west, in the cultural genocide taking place in Tibet. As for the billion people squeezed between these well-known locations? Of them I knew next to nothing.

I was particularly unaware of what life was like for the teenagers I would soon be teaching. The only stories I had read about young people in China were stories of the Great Proletarian Cultural Revolution, a ten-year period lasting from the mid-1960s to the mid-1970s. At the beginning of the Cultural Revolution, a rabidly Maoist army of teenagers—whipped into a quasi-religious fervor by exhortations from the Chairman—enforced an Alice-down-the-rabbit-hole chaos meant to usher in a messianic age of Communist perfection. The kids, who called themselves the Red Guard, were told by the Communist Party that "everything that does not fit the socialist system and proletarian dictatorship should be attacked." Or, as Chairman Mao put it, "To rebel is justified."

High school students, in particular, took this to heart and went completely berserk. Mao issued directives forbidding police to arrest students regardless of their crimes. Young people were also given free transport on trains and buses, and restaurants were required to feed them gratis. Thus, while American teens of the 1960s were tuning in, turning on, and dropping out in a bong-assisted quasi-rebellion, Chinese teens were waving their Little Red Books and engaging in rebellion of a more genuine variety.

It was not a good time to be a teacher: every student with a bone to pick became a deadly threat. Teachers who gave students bad grades risked being accused of deviating from a "strict Maoist line." The most unpopular educators found themselves slapped with the label "capitalist roader." Once these accusations were made there was almost no way to avoid punishment. Foreign teachers were particularly helpless. The lucky ones were deported; others were locked for the decade in cowsheds or sent to rice paddies for reeducation. Chinese nationals had it worse. Thousands were beaten and hundreds killed. There are even accounts of students capturing, flaying, and eating teachers who did not worship Mao with sufficient zeal.

As I sat on the bus, however, stories of teacher kebobs seemed completely unbelievable. I was, after all, looking out the window at what seemed to be a fully modern society. I saw bowling alleys, a Toyota dealership, a planetarium.

A planetarium? Chengdu was going to be full of surprises.

The buildings that zipped past my window were tall and covered in green-tinted glass. Shoppers filled the sidewalks and bike lanes were stacked ten deep with riders grinding away in the now-shimmering heat. Many of them had rigged umbrellas to their handlebars to protect themselves from the sun. Above the sea of umbrellas, advertisements flashed in neon, and models stared down from billboards. Most of the models were scantily clad adolescent girls or shirtless, six-pack-ab boys, flaunting their nipples like talismans. It was an amped up, hyper-polluted, and densely populated version of Times Square.

The stories of cannibalism were therefore at the top of a long list I was compiling in my journal under the heading "No way could this possibly be true." The list had grown as, in the months before my departure, I read more and more about China.

Some highlights from the list:

- Reports that there were 30,000–40,000 full-time Internet censors working in Beijing to maintain the "Great Firewall of China," the Communist Party's national Net Nanny / Big Brother program; other reports that China had surpassed the U.S. as the most wired country on earth (in terms of numbers of users)

- Economic analyses estimating that 400 million Chinese have been lifted out of poverty since 1990, by far the fastest and most widespread reduction in poverty in world history; WHO estimates that despite this, 100 million Chinese are still malnourished and that another 400 million live on less than two dollars a day

- Government studies showing that 50% of China's rivers and lakes are so polluted that they are not even fit for industrial usage and that 90% of China's urban groundwater is contaminated; WHO reports that sixteen of the world's twenty most polluted cities are inside China and that nearly 200 Chinese cities fail to meet minimal air-quality standards; other reports that China has some of the strongest environmental laws in the world

- Tobacco-industry figures showing that Chinese smoke more than twice the number of cigarettes per year than the entire Western Hemisphere (that's 75 packs a year for every man, woman, and child in the country)

- Estimates that there are more lawyers working on an average day in Manhattan than there are across China

- Chinese Communist Party reports that there are 100 times more "public-order disturbances" in China today than there were a decade ago (87,000 such disturbances entered the official record in 2005)

Looking down the list gave me the impression that China was a chaotic, Wild West kind of place. The days of eating teachers were long past, and I felt with reasonable certainty that I would not be stuffed into a dim sum. But what could I expect in my role as a volunteer teacher?

Before joining the Peace Corps, I taught history and English in high schools in New York and New Jersey. I knew American teenagers were a frightening combination of hormones, angst, and AXE body spray. Would my Chinese students be similar? Would they dream of getting rich or of furthering the global socialist revolution? Would they play basketball or ping-pong? Were they Buddhist, Taoist, or atheist? They would know of Karl Marx, but what about more recent Jews of note? What of Jon Stewart, Calvin Klein, or Kyle from Southpark?

Learning about China from the comfort of my couch had taught me some mind-boggling numbers, but I saw no human faces beneath them. It was finally time to find out what life was really like for those beyond the coverage of the American media.

The Land of Two No's

The Peace Corps has been in China for about two decades. The first crop of half a dozen volunteers (or PCVs in the parlance of the organization) was due to begin teaching in September of 1989. Three months before their scheduled arrival, however, tanks rolled into Tiananmen Square and massacred a few thousand people. The June protests that preceded the massacre were part of the largest antigovernment uprising the People's Republic had ever seen, and the Communist Party blamed it in part on "foreign meddling." The Peace Corps was frozen out and the PCVs set to land in Beijing were redirected to other countries. The Communist Party waited for memories of what they called the "June 4th Incident" to fade.

Four years later, in came the volunteers. History works quickly in the PRC.

For a while the Communist Party—still very much suspicious of foreign meddling—limited the Peace Corps to a single, comparatively wealthy, province. PCVs were all placed in Sichuan, which is something like China's California. Parallels abound: both places are economic engines far from the seats of national government; both bring in thousands of migrant workers; both are home to major political figures who reshaped the ideological landscape of their countries in the 1980s (Reagan from California, and Deng Xiaoping—Mao's famous successor—from Sichuan). California is home to the innovations of Silicon Valley. Sichuan is home to Deng's innovation, "Socialism with Chinese Characteristics," a catch-all phrase for China's post-Maoist economic and political system.

A decade after the Peace Corps entered China, as the Tiananmen Square Massacre disappeared from the political landscape, volunteers were allowed into regions far poorer than Sichuan. One such region was Guizhou, a mountainous province at the geographical center of China with a total area equivalent to that of Missouri and a population three times that of New England. The northern half of the province was politically and historically significant: Mao became the chairman of the Communist Party while hiding out in Guizhou, and China's current supreme leader, Hu Jintao, began his political ascent in the bare-knuckle politics of the provincial capital. The southern half of the province was, by contrast, a national joke. It was said that southern Guizhou was "the land of two no's": you couldn't go two days without rain, find a person with two coins in his pocket, or take two steps without bumping into an ethnic minority. The joke had some truth to it. The southern part of the province was rain soaked and subtropical; it was, indeed, among the poorest regions in China; and it was—in theory—politically autonomous, controlled by the Miao, Bouyei, and Dong people rather than China's dominant ethnicity, the Han.

If Sichuan was China's California, Guizhou was something like its Kansas. It was a bellwether of the nation as a whole, a province of what the Chinese call the *laobaixing*, or "old hundred names." In American political terms, it was red China, as opposed to the blue, progressive, latte-sipping China of the coast. In Chinese political terms, it was Red China, a region clinging to Maoism. It was both red and Red. It was not the China of the three hundred million Chinese living in Westernized cities. It was the China of the other billion.

After ten weeks of intensive language training, near-daily inoculations for every conceivable sickness, and head-spinning amounts of paperwork, I was told I would be heading towards this other billion. I would be stationed in the provincial capital—Guiyang—and teach at Guizhou University, the largest school in the province. I felt giddy. As exciting and bizarre and beautifully new as life had been in Chengdu, I knew it would be even more so after my move. I told my parents back home in Philly to take out a map of China and drop a finger right in the middle—that's where I would be living. I would be physically—and in some sense politically and economically—at the heart of the People's Republic.

◈

The night before our departure from Chengdu, the Peace Corps staff threw us a farewell banquet. Zhu Kui, the Peace Corps administrator with oversight of the Guizhou program, gave us a pep talk. "You'll be a great success," she told the dozen PCVs who would be scattered throughout the province. "Just stay flexible and open-minded."

Zhu Kui was a big reason our training had gone smoothly. The person with whom I had the most contact, however, had been my language instructor, Teacher Qing. She put me through language boot camp, and after two months of intense Mandarin, I had mastered a few key sentences: *ting bu dong*, "I don't understand"; *bu yao la jaio*, "I don't want hot pepper"; *wo yao pi jiu*, "I want beer."

Chinese was tough on my brain. It was my first tonal language, and it had given me fits from the first day of training. Teacher Qing's patience was all that had kept me from giving up. She was twenty-five years old and buxom for a Chinese woman, with cherubic cheeks and crooked teeth. She wore sundresses and took secret smoking breaks between morning classes. While teaching, she had the demeanor of a soldier in the People's Liberation Army, though when class ended she would smile easily and offer praise. By the end of our training, I had developed Stockholm Syndrome, the psychological dependence kidnapping victims occasionally feel for their captors. A kind word from Teacher Qing would send me into ecstasy. I secretly loved the criticism even more. Teacher Qing owned me.

During our final class, I did my best to speak only in Chinese. I summarized my learning: *"I know how to speak a little Chinese, but I can't read very many characters; other students are very smart, and can already read many words."* I spoke slowly and carefully, making sure my pronunciation of each word was correct. Teacher Qing glowered at me. I felt a shiver down my spine. "Li Lisan, your pronunciation is incorrect." She used my Chinese name, which she had given me in honor of a Shanghai radical of the 1920s. "You just said, *'I, this water, arrive a little Chinese, egg, ten of me, not this written knife.'*"

Oops.

Despite mistakes like this, my classmates and I were extremely grateful to Teacher Qing. After the farewell banquet, we presented her with a gift: a copy of *The Good Earth*. Each of us wrote a short inscription, and we wrapped the book in a map of the United States. We highlighted our hometowns: Lyn from Chicago; Erin from Bowling Green; Nick from Springfield, Missouri; Autumn from Fresno, California; Li Lisan from Philly. We thought *The Good Earth* would be enjoyable for Qing since it was set in China and written in English by a Chinese-American. I was supposed to read the book in eighth grade but played *The Legend of Zelda* instead, so I didn't know if it was any good.

One of my classmates gave Teacher Qing two additional surprise gifts: copies of Ayn Rand's *Anthem*, and William James's *The Varieties of Religious Experience*. The former is an allegorical diatribe against Communism, and the latter is a classic study of religions and the way people live them. I remember being told to read William James in an Introduction to Religions course at Cornell. This time it was round after round of *DOOM* that got in the way.

I started to worry about Teacher Qing. She wasn't aware of the content of these books and they would likely end up on her shelf gathering dust. What would happen to her if a government official visited her home and found a book written by one the world's great anti-Communists? What would they think if they found William James and came to believe she was studying religion? Would she be punished? Sent to the countryside? Reeducated?

Although I worried that these books could get Teacher Qing into trouble, I was glad to have a chance to hear her opinions on them. Her politics seemed fairly mainstream for a person in the Chinese middle class. She was nondoctrinaire. Her one certainty in politics was this: there were tangible benefits to living in a one-party system. Dictatorship or no, every year of her life had seen impressive economic growth, relative stability, and increasingly positive prospects for the future. The Chinese GDP had doubled in size every six to seven years for as long as she had been alive. More skyscrapers would rise in Chengdu during her ten weeks working for the Peace Corps than had been built in Philadelphia in a generation.

As for repression? She had been a toddler during the Tiananmen Square Massacre and shrugged her shoulders when I mentioned it to her. "I know nothing about that," she said. "It doesn't concern me." Tiananmen Square had the same resonance for Teacher Qing as the Kent State Massacre had for me; both were ancient history.

Instead of focusing on the past, Teacher Qing was living intensely in the present. And the present was pretty good. She had a job she enjoyed, a boyfriend, and money to buy new clothing. She dreamed of moving out of her parents' house, owning a car, having a baby boy, and going to Paris for a shopping spree.

The trip abroad would likely never happen, but the rest of her dreams were in good shape. Because of this, she loved her country and respected its leaders. She had very little reason to rock the boat.

"Run for your life from any man who tells you that money is evil," Ayn Rand wrote. "That sentence is the leper's bell of an approaching looter." Teacher Qing seemed like she would approve of this sentiment, yet she was also a card-carrying member of the Communist Party of China (the CPC), which was, in fact, the largest political party in the world, with over sixty million dues-paying members. Could Teacher Qing become a Communist Ayn Rand disciple? It seemed plausible.

I found a chance to ask her this question as we waited together at the bus stop across the street from our classroom. Teacher Qing was heading home—a trip that would take more than an hour and a half in the bumper-to-bumper rush hour traffic—and I was heading to a nearby restaurant for dinner. We would be on the same bus for a few stops, and I took advantage of our time alone.

"I have a question for you about those two books we gave you," I told Teacher Qing. She was fanning herself with a magazine and humming Céline Dion's "My Heart Will Go On." She raised her eyebrows, and I continued. "Ayn Rand was a famous anti-Communist. I wonder if that will be a problem for you?"

Teacher Qing stopped humming and cleared her throat. "If this writer did not like Communism, it does not bother me," she said after a moment. "Not even all Chinese people like Communism. Many people do not even understand it."

"I thought you might get in trouble for criticizing the Communist Party," I said with some surprise. "Isn't that kind of forbidden here?"

Teacher Qing gave me a stern look, arching her eyebrows and pursing her lips. "I do not criticize the Communist Party. No one who loves China would do that. But our Communist

Party is different from others." Teacher Qing said this last sentence with the same confidence she used when describing grammar points. "As Deng Xiaoping told us, 'To get rich is glorious.' We are better at it than even the Americans!" She laughed and batted her eyes at me. Flirting with Commies, I noted to myself, was hot.

"All of this is thanks to the leadership of the Communist Party and Socialism with Chinese Characteristics," Teacher Qing continued. "We will get rich now and develop and catch the West. Then we can develop true Communism later." *Socialism with Chinese Characteristics.* This was a phrase I would come to know well during my two years in China. Anything, I soon learned, could have Chinese Characteristics, from sex to Harry Potter.

"I'm not too clear on what that means," I responded, "but whether socialism has Chinese characteristics or not, Ayn Rand wouldn't like it."

Teacher Qing shrugged her shoulders. "Ayn Rand is dead and has no power. Anyone without power can say anything they want. It doesn't matter."

So much for my concerns about *Anthem.* I moved on to William James. Surely his love of religion would elicit more of a response. "Religion is too dangerous," Teacher Qing once told me. "We are lucky in China to have the freedom to avoid it." We were sitting alone in our classroom at the time, sticky with sweat from the hundred-degree Chengdu heat. I was eating a pork dumpling, a treat I told her was forbidden to me before arriving in China. This shocked Teacher Qing. "Americans love meat, and are very fat!" she yelled.

"Well," I said, "not all Americans are fat. And I usually don't eat pork." I went on to try to explain what it meant to keep kosher and why I had decided China was not the place for this particular manifestation of my Jewish roots. "I want to integrate as much as I can into Chinese culture," I told her, "and I know

food is a big part of it. So I'll eat whatever my hosts are eating."
It hadn't been an easy decision for me, especially since I was
coming out of years of kosher-inspired, strict vegetarianism.
Still, it felt right.

As we chatted, Qing was fanning herself. I was rubbing my
brow with a cold bottle of Sprite. Both of our faces were flushed.
The air was butter thick with humidity. "It is said that Americans are not as free as they think," she told me after I completed
a quick summary of the kosher laws. She went on to tell me what
her college history textbook taught her about America. "You in
America have too much suffering," she explained, "so you have
too much religion. This is the result of economic capitalism and
inequality." I watched a bead of sweat drip down Qing's neck,
over her collarbone, and under the neckline of her dress. The
heat in the room seemed to turn up another notch and I had
unkosher thoughts. "Here in China," she continued, "we are free
to practice religion as long as we never try to impose it on others.
This is true religious freedom." I watched her lips as she spoke.
"In America, on the other hand, Christianity controls everything." Qing was on a roll. "That is why you cannot eat pork."

Our conversation about the laws of *kashrut* had clearly gone
awry. But at that moment, I was less concerned with clearing up
her confusions than I was with banishing thoughts of a naked
Teacher Qing from my mind. Was it her coffee eyes? Her sundresses? Her displays of authority? I wasn't sure.

I reflected on Qing's ideas about religious freedom as we
waited for the bus. I mentioned William James, and Teacher
Qing sighed. "Religion is false," she told me, echoing her earlier sentiments, "but I am superstitious. Sometimes, I wish to
believe things that are not true." She waved her hand to hail
the approaching 57, remaining silent as we pushed our way onto
the densely packed double-decker. I ended up with her crushed
against my chest and a chubby teenager in a blue and white
school uniform crushed against my back. I felt her breasts push

against me. "Peace Corps," I mumbled to myself in a mantra of innocence. "Peacecorpspeacecorpspeacecorps."

Teacher Qing went on to tell me about the one time she had attended a religious service, held in an illegal "living-room church" in the home of a foreign missionary. "It was boring," she told me. "But I bought a pair of crucifix earrings, which are very fashionable. In fact, for some of my friends, Christianity is the greatest fashion of all."

"I'm sure the missionaries hope it will become more than that," I said.

Teacher Qing blew a few stray hairs out of her eyes and responded with an interesting comparison: "Our China believes that simple things are simple. To be a Christian, you just have to change your ideas. This is simple, like fashion. On the other hand, difficult things are worthwhile, like the college entrance exam, or joining the Communist Party. Joining the party requires tests, inspections, and years of work. Not just anyone can become a Communist."

Teacher Qing paused and her flirtatious look suddenly darkened. "Religion is no real danger here in Chengdu. We are not desperate. I will not worry about William James. But in Guizhou, where the people are poor and backwards, it is a very dangerous addiction." Teacher Qing snapped out of her seriousness as quickly as she had entered it and returned to her coy smile. She batted her eyelashes once again.

The books, it seemed, would not get Teacher Qing into any trouble. They did, however, get to the heart of a major dilemma for all Peace Corps volunteers. Part of our job was to serve the communities into which we had been invited and to serve them in whatever capacity they needed. This required us to put aside our assumptions about what was and was not helpful. We were trained to learn through immersion and listening. Most PCVs twisted themselves in knots to avoid anything resembling the opposite tactic; we were desperate to steer clear of the White

Man's Burden. We could fraternize with the locals, but had to keep our pants on while doing it.

At the same time, we all felt we had something unique to offer. We wanted our communities to learn about America and Americans. We were proud of our country. When were we supposed to bring up the things that made us who we were? When was it appropriate to discuss religion, capitalism, war, or peace? When should we eat what our hosts were eating, and when was it appropriate to keep kosher? When were we supposed to insist that coming to China did not make us feel a cool breeze of religious freedom? When, for that matter, could we let our guard down enough to fall in love?

PCVs worldwide wrestle with these questions (or versions of them). They felt particularly challenging in the closed, hypersensitive confines of Chinese politics. This would be especially true in Guiyang, my soon-to-be home.

"When you arrive in Guizhou," Teacher Qing told me, "you will find people who suffer more than Americans. But even they have not turned to religion!" She laughed as she said this and swept her hair over her shoulder. My heart skipped a beat. Had she slipped a membership card for the Communist Party into my pocket at that moment, I would have signed it in my own blood.

三

Jimmy Is
a Black Boy

Before heading to Guiyang, I was sent with five other volunteers to the far west of Guizhou province for a final week of training. Our task was to provide professional development for two dozen high school and middle school English teachers. They were eager for our arrival: few had ever had a conversation in English.

This was no fault of their own; they were simply too far off the beaten path to have exposure to what they called "authentic conversation." Language classes in the mountains of western Guizhou therefore consisted of listening to Soviet-era tape recordings. "Jimmy is a black boy," one such tape declared in a lilting British accent. "He is not happy. He works day and night, but he gets very little money. . . . In America, the houses for black people are small and poor. Black people in America are cruelly oppressed. Now they are fighting against their oppressors." Students listened to the tape, rose and repeated, and sat back down, cycling through this drill for their daily, hour-long English lesson. In every middle school in the area, twelve-year-olds stood at attention and yelled, "JIMMY IS A BLACK BOY." Local authorities were hoping the Peace Corps could help modernize both the content of lessons like this and the methods used to teach them.

◇

Liupanshui, the largest city in the region, was coal blackened and nestled high in a jagged range of terraced mountains. The city's English moniker was "the city of coolness." This was not because it was a hip place to live; it was because local lakes and high altitude kept the city more temperate than the surrounding areas. We arrived after a brutally hot, twenty-hour, overnight train ride. The fresh air was a welcome reprieve.

The first thing I noticed after exiting the train was the bright blue sky. In the previous ten weeks in Chengdu there had been only two smog-free days. I had become used to pollution so thick you could stare directly at the noonday sun and barely squint. Exiting the train in the mountains, I felt like Gollum emerging from his cave. I was blinded and shocked by the reminder of the power of direct sunlight. As my eyes adjusted, I looked beyond the train station to the mountains hemming in the city. They were lush with foliage and shaped like the drip sandcastles I had made down the Jersey Shore as a kid. The greens and yellows of the mountains offered a stark contrast with the blacks and grays of the city beneath. Liupanshui looked like a bomb had hit it. The buildings were covered in a dark film. Some were crumbling. The roads were rock strewn and sewage flowed in open torrents. The music of jackhammers drowned out any voices that might otherwise have drifted our way. Chengdu was postapocalyptically chaotic, noisy, and dirty. This city was far worse.

We hoofed it from the train station to our hotel, dropped our bags, and headed off to a welcome dinner without pause. Zhu Kui, the Peace Corp's program manager for Guizhou Province, had travelled with us and told us the dinner was "an important lesson in the Chinese banquet."

The banquet. It was already both my favorite and most dreaded moment of cross-cultural interaction. We had attended a number of banquets in Chengdu during our training. Each was a blurry affair in which someone or something was honored, and everyone got blasted. Chinese men, usually buttoned up by cultural expectations of humility and pride, cut loose at the banquets. They drank heavily and implored their American counterparts to do the same. Competitive consumption of kidney-crushing quantities of grain-quality alcohol became a norm. I knew that at these occasions I was entering a minefield of masculinity, race, and etiquette, but as a typical graduate of a large American university (I may as well have minored in beer pong), I couldn't resist avid participation.

Liupanshui banquets would make their Chengdu cousins look tame. Local officials rarely had the opportunity to host foreign guests, and they wanted to make sure they made the most of the encounter. "This week will have many banquets," Zhu Kui explained. "It is important that we participate to let our hosts thank us, but you must be very careful." In an unwitting echo of Nancy Reagan, she went on to warn us to be ready to "just say no." She was particularly concerned since Guizhou was the proud home of the most famous *bijiu* distillery in China, the Maotai brewery. *Bijiu* was simply called "wine" by the Chinese, but it was, in fact, a fiery 100-proof ancestor of Japanese saké. We knew we would be swimming in rivers, lakes, and oceans of the foul liquid. Our week in Liupanshui would be something like a nonstop frat party if it were held in Tequila, Mexico, or on whatever island Captain Morgan calls home. Chengdu, by contrast, offered mild *bijiu* as well as Coca-Cola mixed with red wine, a drink teacher Qing told me was "as fashionable as the crucifix."

For lunch and dinner each day for a week we sat with different configurations of hosts, each trying to outdo the others. Dinner on Monday was with Communist Party officials; on

Tuesday we sat with the local education secretary, a Chinese version of Chris Farley who drank more in an evening than I thought humanly possible; Wednesday found us with the leaders of the local college; Thursday was hosted by the top middle school in the city; Friday was organized by some combination of these groups that I could not untangle.

The hosts for the banquets changed but the ritual did not. Each began with a toast accompanied by a short welcome speech. "You have come to our poor city as friendship volunteers," the official in charge often began. "Thank you for your help. Now please get your freak on."

The last part is a loose translation. More directly, the speech would end with a call of *ganbei*, literally, "dry your glass." A barrage of highly ritualized toasts always ensued. First, each official would approach each American man to offer an individual toast. Women were left out of the required ceremonies. After the officials had each toasted the men, we were free to return the favor. Next, individuals could toast entire tables. This brought more *bijiu*. Finally, there were calls of *ganbei* for the married couples, for all the Americans in the room, for Asian-Americans, for Yao Ming, etc. The nicest thing about Chinese banquets was their relative brevity. After a few hours, everyone was so stinking drunk that it became pointless to continue.

At the final banquet that week, things got out of control. One Communist official sitting at my table was so drunk that his bald head turned the color of the Chinese flag. He told me I looked like Michael Scofield, the protagonist of the then-popular FOX hit *Prison Break*. He told the married volunteers to go back to the hotel and have sex to get their families started. He told us that Chinese women want to "become white like Michael Jackson." He was shoveling food in his mouth, downing shots, and laughing a deep belly laugh for most of the night.

After the banquet was in full swing, the official presented each PCV with a gift. They came in black boxes the size of Nalgene bottles. I opened my box to find a replica of the giant, forty-foot-tall obelisk that stood at the center of Liupanshui. My version was a six-inch phallus that looked a lot like the crystal Superman used to contact Jor-El in the Fortress of Solitude. "This is so you will never forget our city," he told all of us. "*Ganbei!*"

We did another shot. I went momentarily cross-eyed, and the phallus in my hand divided in two. I came close to projectile vomiting on the general secretary of the Liupanshui Teachers College Communist Party. I didn't want to vomit, but I knew that refusing a toast could be insulting. Luckily for me, attention soon turned from drinking to singing. A karaoke machine appeared, and our hosts lined up to take turns serenading us.

The first number came in a warbling falsetto from a student from Liupanshui's top high school. She introduced herself to us with her English name, Smiss, a name I thought I misheard until she spelled it for us to make sure we had it right. Smiss gave us her rendition of "Sweetheart, I Love You," a smash single by the pop star Li Yuchun. During my time in Chengdu I heard the song dozens of times. It was that summer's Chinese equivalent of Mariah Carey's "We Belong Together." Both songs were female power-ballads of the summer of '05, both were embarrassingly catchy, and both had a distinct lack of lyrical creativity. Carey and Li both sang "oh baby, baby," "I need you back in my life," and "oooooh, yeah."

While Li Yuchun's lyrics were mundane, her persona was riveting. She had short, spiked hair, she beat-boxed to begin some of her songs, and she scandalized the nation with her gender-bending sense of style. Her detractors nicknamed her "Spring Brother," teasing her for dodging the narrow standards of Chinese femininity. She responded by giving herself a unisex name in English: Chris Lee. Whatever you called her, she seemed to be channeling David Bowie during his Space Oddity phase. In the surrealist music video for "Sweetheart, I Love You," Li got punched in the face in a boxing match and blown into an ocean, where she was rescued by a pink cartoon rabbit who flew her into a world of clouds. It was as bizarre as it was popular.

Shortly before our arrival in Liupanshui, Li won the *Super Girl* competition, China's version of *American Idol*, making her—at least momentarily—the biggest star in Asia. Her popularity was so intense, in fact, that she spooked the Communist Party. Li's sing-off in the *Super Girl* finale had been the most watched live event in the history of television. Estimates were that a quarter of a billion people tuned in and voted—via text message—for their favorite singer. It was the most democracy China had ever seen and the Communist Party was horrified. *Super Girl* was banned forever.

After Smiss finished singing, we heard a couple of tunes in English. John Denver returned, proving that "Take Me Home, Country Roads" had penetrated far beyond Beijing bathrooms. We also heard the Carpenters classic, "Yesterday Once More." I had no idea why these songs were popular. I made a mental note to try to bring better music to the Chinese people. I would teach them about Bon Jovi and They Might Be Giants.

I spent much of "Yesterday Once More" with my eyes closed, trying to stop the room from spinning. My mind wandered from China to Philadelphia and back. It wandered to Teacher Qing's hemline. I was snapped out of my daydreaming when one of the local officials patted me on the back. "Ms. Zhu Kui tells me you are the Jewish volunteer," he said in perfect English. I tried to bring his face into full focus, but I was still seeing double. I swallowed, hard.

He leaned in close to me and went on, a slight smile on his face. "It is said that in America, the money is in the pockets of the Jews, and the brains are in the heads of the Chinese."

I grunted and blinked. His head was spinning on its axis and I swayed uncontrollably. "That's a new one for me," I told him.

"I greatly admire the Jews," he continued, "but I do not admire

Karl Marx or Trotsky." The man pulled a pack of cigarettes out of his pocket and offered one to me. I took it and tried to balance it on its end on the table. I was too drunk to pull it off.

The man lit his cigarette. "Marxism made us weak. Now that we have abandoned it, we are regaining our proper place in the world." He took a deep drag, leaned back, and blew the smoke out of his nose. He seemed deeply satisfied. "It won't be long before America fades away. You have too many wars. Soon China will have one hundred years of glory. When the Jews begin to immigrate here, we will know we have won!"

I nodded awkwardly, before resting my head on the table and falling fast asleep.

◇

Despite the heavy drinking, the week in Liupanshui felt like a success. It was my first taste of life in the China of the other billion, and I had enjoyed the flavor. Still, the official end of Peace Corps training made me nervous. Was I ready to become a full-time ESL teacher? Could I survive without Teacher Qing, Zhu Kui, and the Peace Corps staff? How would things go for Nick, Erin, Brian, Casey, Mary, Derek, Becca, and my other friends scattered throughout western China? As I boarded the train for Guiyang, the city I would call home for the next two years, I barely had time to formulate answers. I settled onto my bunk and watched the countryside flash by as I travelled due east.

◇

Eight hours later, the train arrived in Guiyang. It was late on Friday evening. Had I been back home in Philadelphia, I would have been sinking into the relaxation of Shabbat, the weekly Jewish holiday of rest, prayer, and study. I would be preparing to walk to synagogue, and my mom would likely be preparing dinner. This Shabbat would be quite a bit different. It would be my first night in my new home.

四

Guizhou University

The main gate of Guizhou University was an imposing fence buttressed by guard towers and adorned with the calligraphy of Mao Zedong. Local legend had it that the Chairman bestowed his penmanship upon the province's flagship school to thank Guizhou for its role in bringing him to power. The main gate was, after all, only a few miles south of the "Zunyi Meeting," the location of one of Mao's greatest leaps forward from humble librarian to supreme dictator. It was at the Zunyi Meeting that Mao wrested control of the Communist Party from his less revolutionary predecessors. This was back in 1935.

Things have changed since those days of Communist guerrilla war. When Mao first entered Guizhou, the province had no rail lines, few paved roads, and only a handful of inhabitants who spoke proper Mandarin. The province was entirely rural. Tiny farms wound along steep mountain paths, and the province's capital and largest city—Guiyang, future home of Guizhou University—was a sleepy trading hub for the indigenous ethnic groups that had long called central and southwestern China their home. The Bouyei, Miao (or, as we call them in the States, Hmong), Hui, and Dong people, along with a smattering of

Tibetans, lived in relative isolation and near-total autonomy, each speaking their own language and following their own religious traditions. The emperors had never bothered to subjugate them fully. There was simply nothing in the region of value or interest.

Once the Communists took over, however, things began to change. Millions of intellectuals, capitalists, and students were relocated to China's backwaters in a movement called the *shangshan xiaxiang yundong*, or "up to the mountains and down to the villages." Chairman Mao believed Communist utopia could only be achieved when the privileged learned from the peasants. Since Guizhou was full of peasants, it became a gigantic reeducation center. Mao thought of its mountains and villages as models of simplicity, poverty, and nonbourgeois values.

One of the "privileged" who was banished to Guizhou was a young intellectual named Wang Bo. He was born in Shanghai to a family of teachers. In 1970, at the age of twenty-two, he was given a choice: go to Guizhou for reeducation and thought reform, or go to jail. He mulled this over for about a week and reluctantly chose Guizhou. Jail was an only slightly less appealing option.

For two years, Wang lived in a tiny farmhouse in the Guizhou countryside. Its straw roof was so thin he could stare through it at night and see the stars. Wang eventually received word that he had "overcome his bourgeois tendencies." He was not yet allowed to move back to Shanghai, but he could find work away from the fields. He decided to move to the most cosmopolitan place the province had to offer and he began teaching in Guiyang.

He never left. Wang was one of the thousands of youths from the *shangshan* movement who settled down in the province, electing to stay even after the campaign came to a close in the mid-1970s. Like many of the transplants, he found that life in the quiet mountains was not as miserable as he had assumed it would be. He enjoyed the clean air, the relaxed lifestyle, and—most of all—he enjoyed being far from the political tumult of the coastal cities. He also found that with his big-city education, he had a leg up on all the local competition. Wang eventually became the dean of the English department at Guizhou University (or Gui Da, as it was known to the locals), and it was he who greeted me at the train station upon my arrival.

"It's nice to meet you," he said in English as he ran forward to greet me on the platform. "You must be our new foreign teacher."

"How did you guess," I joked.

Dean Wang chuckled. "It's true, you're not hard to spot." I was six inches taller than anyone else at the train station. Not to mention much paler.

"Welcome to our Guiyang," Dean Wang bellowed with a smile. His English was thickly accented but still clear enough for me to understand. He grabbed my bag and threw it over his broad shoulders. He had a round, flat face, the body of a retired linebacker, and thick Mr. Magoo glasses. He wore what I recognized as the unofficial uniform of the Chinese yuppie: black pleather shoes, dress slacks, and a textured grey T-shirt, accessorized with a man-purse. Dean Wang seemed immensely happy and his smile was infectious. He laid a calming hand on my back as we walked out of the station towards a waiting car and driver. "I will take you to your apartment, and then I will take you shopping at our Guiyang Walmart."

"Guiyang has a Walmart?" I asked with surprise.

"Our Guiyang has *two* Walmarts!" Dean Wang replied proudly. "We also have a Pizza Hut, so I know you will be very used to life here." I decided not to tell Dean Wang that I had never been to a Walmart back home, and hadn't been to a Pizza Hut since Adam Goldberg's fourteenth birthday party during which he ate so much pepperoni that he vomited into the salad bar. I doubted the Guiyang Pizza Hut would offer an experience to top that.

Dean Wang was walking quickly ahead. I double-timed my pace to catch up. "You start teaching tomorrow morning," he said as we slipped into his car. I didn't know what I would teach, what books I would use, how many students I would have, or how old they would be, but at that moment, none of it mattered. I was sweaty, exhausted, and disheveled, but I felt as happy as Dean Wang looked.

An hour later, we were at the gate of the university. "Chairman Mao wrote this calligraphy," Dean Wang said with pride as he pointed at a six-foot-tall engraving of the school's insignia. I didn't notice the calligraphy; I was staring at the guard towers. Was that to keep local people out, or students in?

The car ride had taken us from the center of town down a six-lane highway to the southern tip of the city. I got a good look at the sprawl of Guiyang, a huge urban area (by American standards) of anywhere from two to three million people, depending on the estimate. Exact numbers were impossible to ascertain due to the constant flow of migrant labor. As in other Chinese cities, you could often recognize these workers at a glance: dark, sun-worn skin, green military pants, and red-white-and-blue rice bags full of clothing, tools, and travel gear. The workers drifted from job to job, sending money back home to their villages in an internal remittance system. They would visit their families only once or twice a year, spending the rest of the time doing construction and traveling by bus, train, and foot. Many students at Guizhou University were children of these migrant laborers, their tuition made possible by the few dollars a day their fathers or mothers were earning in China's urban boom.

Guiyang was certainly participating in the boom: in less than thirty years, the population of the city had doubled, and doubled again. The roads, housing, and infrastructure had not kept pace with the population, but this was not from lack of effort. Construction was everywhere.

Because of this, the city first struck me as chaotic and illogical.

Guiyang seemed to have been poured into the valleys of the Guizhou mountains, creeping and seeping into every available level surface. None of the roads led in a straight line for very long, and alleyways and side streets jutted out at odd angles. At the intersections of most of the major roads, massive pedestrian overpasses sprang out of the sidewalks. At other intersections, tunnels sank the foot traffic beneath the roads, allowing cars and buses to race by unimpeded. The sidewalks, overpasses, and tunnels were wide and densely packed with people. It felt like I was looking at an ant farm and travelling along the surface of an industrial wedding cake. Nighttime in Guiyang was straight out of the Dark Knight's Gotham.

On that first drive down the north-south axis of the city, as we moved away from the center of town, I noticed that the buildings went from high-rise to low-rise, and from new construction to Soviet era. Office towers covered in blue-tinted glass were replaced by squat stone apartments. The traffic thinned a bit, but my knuckles remained white as I gripped the dashboard in front of me. I simply could not understand how we weren't constantly ramming into people, animals, and other cars. No one obeyed lane markings or traffic signals. Oncoming cars veered onto our side of the road without warning. Cows shared the road with buses, VW Jettas, and pedestrians. Honking was constant. I saw cars without bumpers, motorcyclists driving at full speed while carrying babies in their arms, and children driving tractors down the center of the highway. My father—who once spent a summer earning extra cash as a cabbie in New York City—drives like a maniac and has inured me to most bouts of motion sickness. Guiyang traffic, however, was entirely new. I moaned softly for most of the trip.

As we drove, we saw restaurants, factories, schools, and hospitals. A river ran beside the highway and hundreds of older men and women were fishing and washing clothing along its banks. Beyond the river, at the foot of the mountains, were tiny villages. "I used to live in one of those poor places," Dean Wang told me, following my gaze. "They are mostly for the Bouyei people. They are quite backwards."

"Looks like an interesting place to visit," I responded. Dean Wang was taken aback.

"Oh, no," he told me, shaking his head. "You won't like it at all. Too primitive."

I grunted and frowned. "I'm not sure what that means."

"It means those are superstitious people," Dean Wang explained quickly. "You're better off staying on the campus of the school. It is safer for you."

I shrugged. I'd wait a few weeks and visit the village on my own. What Dean Wang didn't know wouldn't hurt him.

五

Moron

The next morning I woke up at dawn, full of teaching-related anxiety. I knew I would never get back to sleep—I was simply too amped up on nervous energy—and decided to head to my classroom. I was surprised to find a student waiting for me. He was standing near the window reading a newspaper. He scurried to my side as soon as he saw me. "You have the shit room," he said before I could introduce myself. These were, in fact, the first words spoken to me in my official capacity as an English teacher at Guizhou University (although to be precise, I should say that the words were *yelled* at me. The student was extremely excited, and everything he said was at full volume). I asked the student his name. "Jackie!" he bellowed, "because my greatest hero is Jackie Chan!" Jackie was short, pudgy, and always spoke with his hands. "This room is convenient," he said, opening his arms in a dramatic gesture, "but malodorous!"

I was impressed with Jackie's English and told him so. He smiled and took his seat. His description of the room was certainly accurate. The walls were neon green and smudged with coal soot. The window panes were cracked or nonexistent. A creaking lectern sat at the front of the room and a poster of Karl Marx hung at an angle over a door that was off its hinges. The overhead lights did not work. Worst of all, the room sat directly across from the men's bathroom—a doorless cave with troughs for both urine and feces. When the wind blew in the wrong direction, my classroom was perfumed with the scent of human waste.

Students slowly filed in on that first day, sleepy eyed and slow afoot. I had not been told how many of them to expect, what books to use, nor the focus of the course. (Literature? Public speaking? Writing? American culture?) I knew only a room number. Dean Wang had assured me that the other information would come to me in due time.

"What should I teach the class?" I asked him during our drive from the train station.

"Teach them to open their mouths." He nodded solemnly as he said this, and I joined him. This I could do.

As the students first saw me, their energy immediately changed. There were gasps, widened eyes, and whispers. "*A foreigner,*" one said to another. "*A foreign* devil," a third corrected. I was standing on the concrete podium at the front of the room getting my notes ready. I had laid out a plan the night before with the aim of being flexible: perhaps I would confront a room of two hundred freshmen who didn't speak a word of English and wanted nothing more from me than a song, or perhaps it would be a small group of nearly fluent graduate students expecting a lecture on Shakespeare. I had experienced plenty of First Days as a teacher, but this was by far my most nerve-racking. Teaching U.S. history at Moorestown Friends School in South Jersey was right up my alley. Teaching American literature at Darrow School—even as a twenty-two-year-old, fresh out of college and only a few years older than some of my students—was no problem. But teaching ESL in a classroom half a world away from home? Teaching a class that included members who thought of me as the spawn of Satan? My nervous energy was tipping towards paralyzing fear.

At 8:00 a.m. on the dot, sixty eyes stared out at me. Or fifty-nine to be more precise. One student was wearing an eye patch. I would later learn that he had lost his eye due to a minor injury. He had gone to the hospital but did not have enough money to pay for the antibiotic eyedrops he needed. In Guizhou, there was no medical insurance and all hospitals required patients to pay up front and in full. If a person couldn't pay he would be refused service. Some patients were left to bleed out in the hospital lobbies. Others lost an eye. It was another strange aspect of a socialist economy with Chinese Characteristics.

The students were gathered on grey particle-board benches with wobbly tables in front of them. Some munched on greasy breakfast buns, looking out at me like chipmunks nibbling nuts and eyeing a predator. Others sat tall, mouths agape. There were twenty-five girls in the class and only five boys. They were all college sophomores.

"Good morning," I began. A chorus responded in loud singsong, "GOOD MORNING!" I was startled by the response, and reminded of stand-and-repeat lessons of Jimmy the Black Boy. The class giggled. I introduced myself and received a round of applause. This startled me even more. Perhaps I wasn't a devil.

I started the lesson.

"To begin our first class, I will introduce myself." Since I wasn't sure of the level of my new students' comprehension, I spoke slowly and enunciated clearly. "At the same time, I will assess your speaking skills." I had the students stand one by one and ask me a question, which I briefly answered. This gave them a chance to get to know me and gave me a chance to hear each of them say something in English. I jotted down a few notes after each of their responses to keep track of words or phonemes that gave them trouble. They ranged in ability from nearly fluent to totally incomprehensible. Jackie, the student who had told me my office was "malodorous," was among the best students, although he continued to yell every word he spoke. At the other end of the spectrum were a few students whose English was worse than my Chinese, including the young man with the eye patch. "I lost my eye," he seemed to say on that first day, though I wasn't sure if I understood him clearly. "What a pity," he continued.

The worst student in the class was a short, muscular young man who had apparently chosen the English name Moron. "Thanks, Moron," I found myself saying when he finished introducing himself. People learning any second language run the risk of accidently choosing old-fashioned or embarrassing names, or names that simply make no sense (Smiss?). The students at Guizhou University were no exception. Moron's name was ridiculous, but it wasn't even close to the strangest of the day. "Anvil," a butch girl with a bowl cut, had already introduced herself, as had an effeminate boy who went by "Dandy." Two skinny girls sitting next to each other in the front row had introduced themselves in unison as "Shitty" and "Pussy." Shitty explained her name by telling me that it "sounded friendly." Pussy told me she liked cats. My fellow PCVs taught students with names that were even more bizarre: Shmily—which, the student explained, stood for See How Much I Love You; Larple— "I am a little fat," she told her teacher, "like a large apple"; God, Red Hero, and Waiting G; and a pair of best friends named Stone and Stone Crusher.

Jackie raised his hand after Moron sat down. "His name is 'Gordon,' Mr. Mike, not 'Moron!' " Jackie yelled. "But his English is very poor so you cannot understand him!" Jackie was looking sternly at Gordon. "His Chinese is very poor, too! He is a minority person, so he has difficulty learning!"

"Well, Jackie," I said, shocked at this seemingly racist comment. "That's . . ." I bit my lip and paused. What had Jackie meant by what he said?

"Well, Jackie," I repeated, "I'm a minority person, too." Gordon, who had been hanging his head as Jackie criticized him, looked up at me. "I'm Jewish," I went on, "one of America's minority groups." No one seemed to understand, so I switched to Chinese. "*Wo shi youtairen*." This elicited a collective "oh!" from the class. I was a person who was special, too.

"Jews are very clever," said Li Dong Mei, a strikingly beautiful student staring at me intently from the front row. She was one of a handful of people in the class who had chosen to keep their Chinese names.

"Karl Marx was a Jew," said the girl sitting next to Jackie. She had introduced herself earlier, with nearly flawless pronunciation, as Yvette Chen.

"Einstein was also a Jew," said Pussy. Shitty nodded in agreement.

Gordon was smiling now, his previous shame replaced by a look somewhere between confusion and pride. I told the class we could talk more about Judaism later, but for now we should continue the lesson. Marx and Einstein, it seemed, would be at my side for as long as I was in China.

When class ended, most students shuffled quickly past me and out into the hallway. One young man lingered behind, and as I wiped chalk from my hands he slowly approached me. He was tall with close-cropped hair. He walked ramrod straight, and had the chin of a People's Liberation Army poster child. "Good morning," he said to me quietly. His voice was soft, but his eyes were confident. He had already introduced himself, and I greeted him by name: "Good morning, Kevin. What can I do for you?"

Kevin handed me a piece of paper. He presented it to me with both hands, a polite gesture which I reciprocated by receiving the paper with both hands. The paper was lined and rowed, and full of Chinese characters. I could read none of it. "What's this?" I asked.

"It is the class roster. I am the class monitor, so it is my job to keep track of everyone."

Kevin was still standing at attention, legs together, chin held high. "At ease," I told him. He looked at me quizzically. "Never mind," I said with a chuckle. "Do me a favor, Kevin, and write these names in English so that I can read them. I can't really read much Chinese yet."

Kevin nodded. "It is no problem. You can tell me anything else you need. If the students cause trouble, I will prevent it. I am proud to be the monitor."

"That's great," I told Kevin. Before I could ask more about his position, he had followed his classmates out the door.

六

My Mr. Belvedere

My apartment was on the second floor of a four-story cinder-block complex that housed most of Guizhou University's retired teachers. The massive compound had been built in the 1950s with the aid of Soviet advisors. It had not been renovated since.

The retired teachers didn't complain, however, since their housing was free. Guizhou University, like Guizhou in general, was still clinging to Mao's idea of the "iron rice bowl." Up until the mid-1980s, when Deng Xiaoping's economic reforms wiped out the Maoist model, everything was provided to Chinese workers (or teachers, in this case) by their work unit, or *danwei*. They received housing, food, health care, child care, and schooling from their employer. They could even expect managers and administrators to match them with a spouse. In exchange for this security, workers surrendered freedom and mobility. They were tied to their job for life, living at the whim of their superiors. They could not even search for a new job without permission from their bosses.

This cradle-to-grave dependence and security—all of which was once thought of as an unbreakable, iron-clad (or iron-bowled) guarantee from the Communist Party—were long dead in the wealthier regions of China. Deng's "Opening and Reform" liberalized and decentralized the economy. The result was "Socialism with Chinese Characteristics."

At Guizhou University, however, the retired teachers, many of whom had been longtime members of the Communist Party, and a handful of whom had even met Chairman Mao in the days of the Zunyi Meeting, made sure their *danwei* continued to function. They had accumulated vast amounts of *guanxi*, the hidden power that ran China. *Guanxi* means, quite simply, "relationships." Without *guanxi*, getting anything done in the byzantine world of Guizhou politics was impossible. The old teachers had fingers on enough buttons and had accumulated enough chits to make sure their iron rice bowls remained intact. They didn't want Chinese Characteristics. They wanted plain old socialism.

In part, they had it. Their apartments were guaranteed for life, rent free; they ate for free at the campus dining hall; they had lifetime memberships at the university bathhouses. "Guiyang is not as rich as Shanghai, or certainly not as rich as America," Dean Wang would one day tell me as we walked past a group of retirees entering the bathhouse. "But we will still always thank Chairman Mao and the party for giving us the *danwei*." He gave me his usual slap on the back. "Money isn't everything! People here have never had much, but at least in my time, what we've had, we've shared."

Dean Wang recognized that this ethos was dying fast. As I got to know my new school, however, I experienced a campus that felt more like a community than any I had visited in America. Children played soccer in a primary school at the center of campus; middle-aged women walked slowly, seeking out one neighbor or another for a brief tête-à-tête; groups of old men sat on their stoops playing mahjong. Three generations were often outside enjoying the sun and interacting.

The last time I had experienced a similar feeling of community had been in the summer of 2000. In July of that year I moved to Jerusalem. I went seeking a deeper connection to Judaism and studied for the year at a yeshiva located not far from the Old City and the Western Wall. My mornings and afternoons were spent reading Torah and Talmud, my evenings were spent in dim clubs full of cigarette smoke, cheap beer, and falafel breath. I tried as hard as I could to do the following, in no particular order: discover God; pick up curvaceous Israeli women; learn Hebrew; get away from American culture and the pressures of life back home.

My experiment went well for a while. I loved Jerusalem and the feeling of being spiritually at home. I enjoyed the pace of life, the food, and the texts I studied. I relished the daily nap built into the yeshiva schedule.

My comfort didn't last long. About three months into my stay in Jerusalem, a couple of buses blew up not far from my apartment in Rehavia. All hell broke loose. I cut my study short and moved back to Philly, losing the feeling of community but gaining a feeling of safety. On September 1, 2001, I moved to New York City to start graduate school. Ten days later . . . well, I was out of the frying pan and into the other frying pan.

It was 9/11 that inspired me to join the Peace Corps. On September 12th, like many others, I swore to myself that I would serve my country. *I'll join the army,* I thought. When I mentioned this to my mother, she reminded me that splinters and hangnails made me woozy. I realized that a person who can't even watch boxing matches out of fear of the violence might not be cut out for combat. I am as metrosexual as they come.

There was, however, an alternative to the Marine Corps. The Peace Corps. It, like the military, offered me a sense of doing something, an illusion of control, and by the end of that shocking September, I had promised myself I would join. Four years later I was in China.

This journey—from Philly to Jerusalem to New York to

Guiyang—flooded my thoughts as I stood outside my new apartment. I was a long way from the Upper West Side and a long way from the Kotel. Yet I somehow felt more at home than I had in years. I immediately fell in love with my new neighborhood.

◇

I also liked my new digs. My apartment had three rooms, pink tiled floors, and a six-square-foot closet that functioned as a shower/toilet. The hole in the ground was both a drain and a target for my slowly improving squats. I was learning that if I kept my arms extended in front of me as a counterbalance, I could get close enough to the ground to make a reasonably clean delivery. With each passing day, I was becoming more flexible.

Beyond the bathroom was the bedroom. It was quiet, cool, and dominated by a queen-size bed. The living room was spacious and breezy and contained a small refrigerator, a clothesline, and two couches. The "kitchen" was a low shelf with a plug-in stove on top. Along with the stove, the school gave me a pot and a pan. The pan was moldy, and the pot melted into a puddle of plastic and cheap metal the first time I tried to boil some water. I called Dean Wang in a panic, upset that I had ruined something given to me in a spirit of generosity. "Don't worry," he told me. "I'll send Mr. Ma."

"Who is Mr. Ma?" I asked.

"You have met him," Dean Wang told me. "He is the driver for the foreign-language department. He drove us from the train station."

I was confused. "The driver? It sounds like he is a departmental chauffeur."

Dean Wang chuckled. "Yes. All the departments in the school have drivers. It is a common job in China."

"I didn't know that," I said, resting the phone on my shoulder. "Having a chauffeur in America is pretty rare." Knowing that Mr.

Ma was a full-time driver did not help me understand why Dean Wang was sending him to fix my melted pot. I asked if Mr. Ma had any expertise in this area.

"It doesn't matter," Dean Wang replied. "I will send him to inspect."

Mr. Ma arrived a few hours later. We did our best to communicate, but he spoke only the local Guizhou dialect, a version of Mandarin that at that point I could not understand. All Chinese use the same written characters, but once they begin pronouncing them it's a shit show. Guizhou dialect was not as challenging as, say, Shanghai dialect, and certainly not as unique as Cantonese, but it was still far enough away from standard Mandarin to baffle me. Mr. Ma and I were forced to pass a dictionary back and forth between us pointing at entries in Chinese. He flipped through it for a few minutes, eventually pointing to three characters: 男管家. The phrase, pronounced *nan guan jia*, meant "man pipe house." I was befuddled.

"What's a man-pipe-house?" I asked Mr. Ma in Mandarin. He shook his head and indicated with a chop of his hand that the characters were not to be read separately; they were a single phrase. I went back into the dictionary and found a new word: *butler*. Mr. Ma was claiming to be my Mr. Belvedere. "This doesn't make any sense," I told him. Mr. Ma shrugged his shoulders. I thought of the Green Hornet's kung fu assistant, Kato, played in the 1960s by Bruce Lee. Was Mr. Ma my kung fu assistant?

Unlikely. As I stared at him, he lit a cigarette, wheezed, and smiled at me with brown teeth. I would follow up with Dean Wang for clarity, but at that moment, *nan guan jia* would have to do. With more help from the dictionary, high-quality bodylanguage, and an hour of hard work, Mr. Ma went on to explain that he had a lot of free time on his hands. Our trip from the train station had, in fact, been his first full day of work in months. Not that this mattered; despite having very little to do,

Mr. Ma had no fear of losing his job. He was untouchable, a relic from the days of Maoist bureaucracy when jobs were created with no regard for actual need. "I have my iron rice bowl," he said, in one of the few sentences I understood clearly. He coughed with satisfaction.

Mr. Ma was a driver with no one to drive. He spent days, weeks, even months at a time sitting in the foreign-language department smoking pack after pack of Panda-brand cigarettes, playing Minesweeper on an old PC, and pulling in a government salary. Dean Wang had decided that Mr. Ma could fill some of his time assisting the new foreign teacher. He wasn't exactly a *nan guan jia*, but when something broke, Mr. Ma would be sent over to try to fix it. He had no repair skills I could recognize (and he certainly had no Kato-like kung fu). His solution for the melted pot was to sprinkle it with dirt, stick it under my couch, and never speak of it again. He was even more helpless when he heard the results of my first attempt to use the shower: it dripped sewage instead of spraying water. Mr. Ma engaged in another "inspection."

He began by looking things over in the bathroom. He grunted and looked at me the way I look at a puppy that has had an accident: it's both endearing and annoying to be needed by a helpless animal. He left the apartment and went incognito for a week, leaving me with no option other than to bathe next to the kitchen sink. When Mr. Ma returned, he had a hammer, a wrench, and an odd assortment of pieces of plastic. He used the wrench to remove part of the shower apparatus. It immediately began spraying him, the bathroom, and the hallway with foul-smelling water. He screamed, trying to cover the source of the water with his hand. This, of course, only increased the intensity of the stream. He barked at me, gesturing wildly, but I could not understand exactly what he wanted me to do. I improvised by running around the house gathering towels, blankets, and clothing to try to keep the water at bay. Mr. Ma found this absurd, and began slamming the shower against the wall of the bathroom as if it were a living, disobedient animal he could render unconscious. We did not make a good team.

Thirty minutes later, the house was an inch deep in dirty water and Mr. Ma was soaking wet, but the shower was repaired. Or somewhat repaired. He had attached the replacement parts backwards and upside down so I had to reach behind a burning-hot pipe to turn the water on and off. I was mildly thankful.

Pots melted, showers broke, and water flowed. Still, with the addition of some photos on the walls and a few Tibetan tapestries, the apartment started to feel like home. It would never be cozy, but it ended up with a décor that might be called cinder-block chic.

Whatever the apartment lacked in style, it more than made up for in convenience. It was just inside the main gate of the university and only a short walk to my classroom. I fell into a comfortable routine.

My days would begin early with a cup of *pu er* tea, grown in the mountains not far from the city. Sleeping in was never an option since one of my neighbors woke up each morning and sang at the top of his lungs. Through the paper-thin walls of the apartment compound, he sounded like a cat in heat. I wasn't sure what he was singing or why he had to do it so early, but with his help I was always out the door by 7:30. I would head for my classroom, stopping along the way on most mornings to buy a banana or an apple from a farmer who set up a small stand in the alley. If I had a few minutes extra, I would duck into an adjacent alley and buy a freshly fried strip of dough called a *you tiao*. I'd take a few minutes to eat my breakfast and then head towards the center of campus.

The daily walk took me through the courtyard of some newer buildings, past the campus dining hall and student bathhouse, and up a hill. Both the dining hall and bathhouse were usually busy in those early morning hours as students got ready for school. The dormitories—in which students slept eight to ten in a room—had no kitchens or bathrooms of their own. At the top of the hill was a pair of outdoor basketball courts. The courts were asymmetrical and the rims were crooked and net free. Nevertheless, students played from sunrise until well after sunset. They played in the scorching heat, in the rain, and eventually in the dead of winter. I began itching for a game and promised myself I would lace up my sneakers and get out on the court as soon as I had a handle on my classes and felt like they were running smoothly. I had no idea at that point how important basketball would become for both my sanity and my relevance to Guizhou University.

Beyond the courts was Big Building One, a twelve-story architectural monstrosity that housed most of the school's humanities departments. It looked like something straight out of *TRON*. The Foreign Language Building, older and ivy covered, sat in Big Building One's shadow. It contained my office which, like my classroom, sat within smelling distance of the men's bathroom. I could always tell how my day would go by testing to see which way the wind was blowing. An easterly breeze never boded well.

七

Great Jew

A month into my new life, things were running smoothly. I felt I had everything under control. Classes were fun, my Chinese was improving rapidly, and I felt more and more at home in my neighborhood. One morning I watched five adorable kids gather in a small circle not far from my front door. They all had short haircuts, stained T-shirts, and plastic sandals. I decided to test my language skills and attempt an introduction. I sauntered over.

"*Ni hao*," I said, approaching their circle. The children were shocked to see a foreigner towering over them but not nearly as surprised as I was when I saw the game they were playing. One of the boys had tied a small rock to a string, and the boys were using the device to smash a fist-sized bullfrog to death. Each was taking a turn spinning the rock before bringing it down on the frog. It was injured, bleeding, breathing heavily, and doing its best to escape.

I stared at the frog, then at the boys. Their faces registered surprise and guilt. Not only were they caught in the act, they were caught by an odd-looking, sweaty white man.

"What are you doing?" I asked, pleased that my Chinese wasn't failing me.

"We are playing a game," said the leader of the boys. His head was shaved, other than a six-inch tail running from the base of his skull. It was a haircut I had unfortunately shared at his age. It was a lousy haircut in 1985, and seemed even worse twenty years later.

"I don't think the frog likes this game," I said. The boys hung their heads. A successful interaction!

The boy with the tail suddenly looked up at me, smirked, raised his foot high off the ground, and stomped on the bullfrog. It exploded in a burst of guts and blood. The five boys screeched with excitement and ran away. I was too stunned to move or speak. I looked down at the remnants of the frog. It was a harsh lesson in the limits of my understanding.

◇

Things were going better with my students than they were with neighborhood children. I had yet to suffer a pedagogical stomping to compare with the frog death. Nevertheless, I was often a step or two behind. Later that day, Yvette Chen—the student who had reminded me that Karl Marx was a Jew—came to visit me during my office hours. I had been holding these open meetings twice a week. They were a big hit. Some students would visit simply to stare at me, but others came to practice their speaking and listening. There were even a few teachers making regular appearances, and, as word spread, students from other universities, high schools, and middle schools began finding their way to Gui Da to get a taste of the authentic English conversation they had never before heard. My office hours were usually rollicking, cramped, and often involved debate, singing, or cardplaying. I was especially fond of Kill the Landlord, a poker-rummy hybrid that Teacher Qing taught me during training in Chengdu. I made a fierce landlord.

On the day Yvette visited my office, it was packed. I had an old wooden couch and a few folding chairs pushed against the walls, all of which were full. Late arrivals were standing in the center of the office and a few were spilling out into the hallway. A handful of others gathered outside the window, leaning in. When Yvette arrived, I was sitting at my desk with Pussy standing next to me. We were in the midst of a long discussion about her name.

"I like my English name," she told me, "but my classmates do not. Maybe you can tell me what to call myself?"

The request made me uncomfortable. Some Peace Corps volunteers required their students to adopt English names. Others found that naming their students felt vaguely imperialistic. Naming is, after all, an intensely personal and powerful act. I fell in the second category.

Still, if a student came to ask for a suggestion, I was willing to listen. Pussy noticed I often smiled when I heard her name. She came to my office hour to ask why. "It's not a name I have ever heard," I told her honestly, "and it sounds funny to me."

"Does 'pussy' have a special meaning?" she asked.

I coughed to mask a laugh. How to respond? I wanted to be frank, but there was no reason to embarrass Pussy for her innocence. "Yes, your name has a special meaning," I told her, once I caught my breath. "As you know, it can mean 'cat,' but it can also be the name for . . ." I paused trying to guess what word would be most appropriate. "It can also be the name for a woman's special area."

Pussy looked at me blankly. Everyone in the office looked at me blankly. Perhaps I was being too coy; these were, after all, college-age students.

"You are named for a vagina," I blurted. Still, there were blank stares. Perhaps anatomy was not in the vocabulary lessons that accompanied the Jimmy the Black Boy curriculum. This would only make sense—there was no such thing as sex ed in China, so why learn about genitals in English?

I grabbed my dictionary and flipped it open. The first entry I found was *shinü*, which literally translated as *rock woman*. "You are named for a *shinü*," I told Pussy.

She screamed. Two people fled the office. "This cannot be," Yvette told me, looking at my dictionary. She pointed to the definition of *shinü*, and I read more carefully: "A woman with a hypoplastic vagina."

"Mike, I think you mean she is named *yindao*." Yvette flipped to another entry in the dictionary. I nodded as I looked at this entry. *Yin* meant woman. *Dao* meant road. This made much more sense.

Pussy was mortified and blushing but had enough composure to stop screaming. "Please suggest a change," she said simply. I told her to call herself Kitten.

I had renamed my first student. I felt unsure about the decision, but not for long. A few days later, a fellow Peace Corps volunteer in Guiyang—a mustachioed Oregonian named Dylan whom I respected immensely—also altered his naming-is-imperialism policy. "I met a student named 'Hitler' today," he told me on the phone. "So I'm dropping the whole no-name-change thing." Dylan decided his student could no longer be Hitler. He forced him to change his name to Moses.

◈

Once Kitten was set with her new name, Yvette stepped forward. She handed me a letter. Its title, announced in bold print along the top of the page, was "GREAT JEW." The letter summarized the status of world Jewry:

Jew in the world:

There are 14 million Jews in the world, 5 million of them are in the Israel, and 6 million in the USA. They have done so many great things for people in the world. They good at jokes, doing business and managing money so that there are a large number of Jewish tycoon in the world. . . . In the Wall Street which is the controlling financial interests of the United States, it is the world of Jews who dominate the "street." Jews deserve careful study though their history is pitiful.

Yvette also included a bullet-point list of facts she had gleaned from her textbooks and from local newspapers:

- Einstein is the greatest scientist in the world
- Every Jew has received high education for their family tradition
- Jews can begin law school in the second year in America, because they are advanced in law
- Phelps, a swimming Jew, will win many gold medals in the Beijing Olympic Games

Yvette told me she was preparing for a speech contest and had chosen Jews as her topic. "I know you are a Jew," she said as she pushed her red-framed glasses up her nose. "Can you help me edit this speech, and also help me include the important facts?"

"Yvette . . ." I said, searching for an appropriate response. Michael Phelps a Jew? "Yvette . . ." I repeated before pausing again. We are good at jokes?

"Listen," I finally said, having failed to find a sensitive way to correct her work. "This is absurd. It's totally unusable."

Yvette, like all Chinese students, was used to harsh criticism. She smiled and blinked at me. "But," she told me, "we have learned it."

"What does that mean?" I said, slightly exasperated. "You've learned it, but it's wrong." Yvette's smile remained sweet and patient.

"It is in a book," she told me.

Before we could get any further, Jennifer He, a bubbly Guizhou native who stood no taller than four foot eleven, burst into the room. Jennifer had wavy hair that flowed down to her waist, carefully applied makeup, and stiletto knee-high boots. She was a fellow teacher in the English department as well as a Guizhou University alum, and over her thirty-plus years in Guiyang she had cultivated friends in high places and developed an impressive amount of *guanxi*. I knew that despite her constant smile and diminutive stature she was no one to be trifled with. Jennifer had been assigned as my "mentor teacher," a job she was taking quite seriously.

"I have good news," she declared, stepping right in front of Yvette and waving a piece of paper in my face. Due to her height, Jennifer had to extend her arm to full length and rise onto her toes to maximize the potential to annoy me with this gesture. "We have created the Guizhou University Jewish Friday Night English and Cooking Corner Club. You will be the leader of the club!" The paper fluttered before my eyes until I snatched it out of her hand.

"Gee, that's wonderful," I muttered. I scanned the paper and saw it had been stamped with the red stamps of both Dean Wang and the top dog at the university, a hard-drinking sixty-year-old named Lu Ping. President Lu insisted that I call him President Bill because, as he told me, "President Bill Clinton is the greatest man in America."

The club was, apparently, something of a big deal. I slumped into my chair as Jennifer and Yvette began an animated discussion in lightning-fast Chinese. Jennifer soon turned to me. "We have just decided that Yvette will be your student leader. Our first meeting is tonight, and President Bill will be there, so don't be late!"

I nodded. G.U.J.F.N.E.C.C.C was born.

八

Squishy Like Mud

Shabbat with the G.U.J.F.N.E.C.C.C. (or the Guj, as I began calling it) would be far different from Shabbat back in Philly or Jerusalem. The word "Shabbat" comes from the Hebrew root meaning "to cease, end, or rest," and in observant Jewish communities, modern life comes to a halt. Lights are not turned on, cars are not driven, heavy loads are not carried. In fact, the rabbis of old created thirty-nine separate categories of activities forbidden on the Sabbath day (including "flaying," "selecting," and "tearing down a building"). Rest, as I later explained to members of the Guj, requires work in Judaism, and lots of it: you have to work hard just to understand what "work" even means.

During Guj meetings, all of this was irrelevant. We would cook Jewish food no matter what Rabbinic rules were broken.

Club meetings were held in Jennifer's damp, fifth-floor apartment which she shared with another one of our colleagues, Vivian Zhou. Both Jennifer and Vivian were born after Mao's death and had grown up as Deng Xiaoping's economic reforms ended the guarantees of the iron rice bowl. They were part of a more laissez-faire generation, a group that was personally unfamiliar with—and somewhat wistful about—the ideas of Mao's heyday. They were not given housing by the university, and unlike their older colleagues, they had never expected this manifestation of government largesse. Instead, the roommates rented their apartment. The three-bedroom, one-bathroom flat cost them the equivalent of twenty-five dollars each month. They were living in a convenient, trendy part of Huaxi, and the building was only a few years old. It was significantly nicer than my digs in university housing.

"Do you wish you had a powerful *danwei*?" I once asked them. With a *danwei*, they would have lived rent free.

Jennifer laughed. "That is impossible now," she said. "Our government has chosen a new direction."

"Well, do you like the new direction?"

Jennifer blinked at me. "It doesn't matter. It has been chosen."

Vivian was a little more thoughtful about her life without an iron rice bowl, though I still found her ideas confusing. "It would be nice to know our apartment would always be ours, like in the old days when the party owned everything," she told me. "But today, it is different. Jennifer and I rent this apartment together, but the government or school can take it whenever they need it. We never know what will happen, and everything is changeable."

Vivian's uncertainty about her apartment was emblematic of a general state of confusion about property law in Guiyang. Residents had to be prepared to move at a moment's notice. I saw this firsthand when one Saturday night I went with Jennifer and Vivian to what they assured me was the best hot-pot restaurant in town. They had made reservations the night before, but when we arrived, the restaurant was closed. It had the familiar Chinese character 拆 spray-painted on its doors. 拆 was one of the first characters I had learned to recognize and it was ubiquitous in some parts of Guiyang. It meant, simply, "tear down." Migrant workers were on the roof of the building smashing it with sledgehammers. The owner of the restaurant emerged to apologize to us. "Sorry," he said with a shrug. "We got word this morning that the government wants the building." The owner was taking reservations for his successful restaurant on a Friday night, and was told to vacate the premises on Saturday morning. He would receive some small form of remuneration, but as he said to us, "We will be forced to move far away. Our business will certainly suffer."

"I don't want a *danwei*, because I love my freedom," Vivian concluded. "But I hate this new world we live in. Everything makes no sense." Jennifer frowned as Vivian made these comments, and remained silent. She was clearly upset, but it would be more than a year before I learned why.

Jennifer's and Vivian's explanations of life in the new China said a lot about their personalities. They were a bit of an odd couple. Where Jennifer was ebullient, well groomed, and crass, Vivian was introspective, schlumpy, and morose. Vivian had small eyes and a beautiful smile. She was one of the few women in our department who had neither permed nor colored her hair. "I know that a woman's beauty is her only hope," she told me, "but right now I just don't care what people think of me." Where Jennifer preferred faux designer clothing and high-heeled leather boots, Vivian went for the understated and simple. This Bert-and-Ernie pair had lived together since their days as undergraduates at Gui Da. They still ate nearly all their meals together, travelled together, and, at times, even finished each other's sentences.

My two new friends were nearly the same age as the only other twenty-something Chinese woman I had gotten to know—Teacher Qing—and they initially struck me as her peers. As time passed, however, I came to realize the only similarity the women had was their nationality. They were as different as Parisians and Chisinauans (the latter being the citizens of one of Europe's lesser-known capital cities), or at least as different as

Carrie Bradshaw and Nicki Grant. Teacher Qing was from West-ernized, wealthy Chengdu, after all, while Jennifer and Vivian were from an altogether different China. I was learning how much different the world looked to women left out of the China boom.

For the first few Guj meetings, Vivian would politely watch us knead challah dough for a few minutes before finding an excuse to lock herself in her room. Jennifer, on the other hand, held court. She had created the club because she wanted to aug-ment her teaching salary with a side business. She figured that since I was Jewish, I would be a good source for advice. Vivian slowly began participating actively in the Guj as well, though it was not to learn my Jewish business secrets. Instead, she simply saw how much fun we were having. "Shabbat," she would later tell me, "is the only happiness I feel each week." Teacher Qing believed religion was dangerous in Guizhou because poverty made the people susceptible to its messages. Perhaps she had been right.

Another participant in the first Guj meeting was President Bill, who, as promised, came knocking on Jennifer and Vivian's door. He treated the occasion as a banquet and brought a gigan-tic white jug of Maotai. "We will drink together," he told me with a wink. He was ready to build some *guanxi* with the new foreign teacher.

The Maotai ensured that the first Guj meeting went by like a blur. I tried to teach the group some Shabbat-appropriate vocab-ulary (*l'chaim*, for example), but it was no use. After less than half an hour, everyone was drunk. Guests started trickling out of the apartment. By 9:00 p.m., it was just me and the president. We were sitting at a small table in Jennifer and Vivian's living room. Jennifer had hung on longer than the other guests, but eventually she, too, had given up and gone to sleep.

"The others are weak," President Bill told me. "They are *lan zui ru ni*." This, translated literally, meant *squishy like mud,* and referred to the effete weakness men in Guiyang attached to those who could not hold their alcohol. "But you, Mike," he continued, "you are strong." President Bill was three sheets to the wind and slurring his words. His face was a sheen of salt and grease and he had rolled up the legs of his pants and his shirt. His belly jiggled before me.

As the booze loosened our tongues, President Bill and I began a blunt conversation about the students at Gui Da. "Our university is very poor," he told me, "and our students are not very motivated." I deflected this negative assessment, but President Bill would have none of it. "Don't think I'm blaming them," he said with a wave of his hand. "I know it isn't their fault. We just don't have an education system that works very well. Everyone knows Chinese are good at math and science, but we are also very bad at creativity. We only build things in factories, but we never innovate and invent them on our own." President Bill was looking at me earnestly. His criticism did not seem bitter and he was not at all embarrassed. "No Chinese citizen has ever won a Nobel Prize," he went on, shaking his head. "Why is this? It is because we only teach the students how to memorize, and we test them and test them, and punish them if they cannot pass the tests. This is why you are at our school. You must teach the students to think."

I told the president I would do my best. (Five years later, Liu Xiaobo would become China's first Nobel laureate, winning the Peace Prize for promoting human rights, democracy, and political freedom in China. His reward? An eleven-year prison sentence for "inciting subversion of state power." I doubted it was this sort of thinking President Bill hoped I would encourage.) President Bill patted me on the back, poured another shot, and asked me why I had chosen to come to Guiyang. I admitted to him that I had been assigned to Guiyang and that I had never heard of the city before my arrival in China. He was shocked.

"But we have a Walmart!" For President Bill, this marked his city as a real comer. "How can you have learned nothing of our city and our province?" he asked me. He gave his belly a hardy slap, spraying sweat for a few yards in each direction. I grimaced, fearing some of the drops had landed in my glass of Maotai. I hoped the 120-proof would be strong enough to kill any sweat-born bacteria.

There would only be a few shots left, regardless. President Bill had an ample girth and a reputation for being one of Guiyang's better drinkers, but he was having trouble keeping up with me. After our first shot of Maotai, more than an hour ago, President Bill's face turned bright red. After the third, his left cheek started twitching and his eyes began watering. After the sixth, his breath became raspy. Nevertheless, he was determined to outdo the foreigner. I felt pity for the man, but I would not yield. Someone was going to lose face.

As we did another shot, President Bill was far enough out of his mind to forgo any of the normal niceties that you might expect when first meeting a new foreign teacher. "You must return to America and teach your shit-for-brains people to love Guiyang." He was stuck on the theme of American ignorance of his hometown. "I have been to America!" he bellowed. "Could I understand your culture if I only saw New York City? Could I understand George Bush if I only visited San Francisco?" He went on like this for some time before falling asleep on the table, cigarette still dangling from his bottom lip. I quietly stood, snuffed out his cigarette, and stumbled home.

九

Our Wonderful Campus

A few months into life at Gui Da and I finally met my singing neighbor. "It's Sichuan opera," he explained to me one afternoon in the alley outside our stairwell. I was returning home from classes, and he was tending to an orange-beaked bird in a wicker cage suspended from the low branch of a tree. "We call it *Chuan ju*. You probably haven't heard of it. Americans all prefer Peking Opera, but *Chuan ju* is much more special."

"Why do you practice in the morning?" I asked, in an attempt at tact. His 6:30 a.m. start times never failed to wake me up.

He brushed the question aside: "When I was younger, not only would I sing, I would face-change and fire-spit. But no one wants to see the opera anymore. Students today spend their time in Internet cafés, or watching movies. China is changing too quickly. What a waste!" The old man was feeding his bird sunflower seeds, one by one. "Have you ever seen Sichuan opera?"

"No," I replied. "But I've certainly heard a lot of it."

At this, my neighbor laughed. He looked down at his slippered feet and shuffled them for a moment. "I suppose it's a little bit loud for the early morning." He nodded and seemed to come to a conclusion: "I will use less gong as I practice, and more *muqin*. That should be more pleasant for you." The *muqin* was a harplike instrument that, along with a gong, served as the standard accompaniment to Sichuan opera. At times I found the long, falsetto notes of the *muqin* beautiful. At 6:30 a.m., I found that they enraged me. Still, I nodded at my neighbor. "I look forward to waking up to your *muqin*," I told him with a frown. He continued feeding his bird.

The *muqin* alarm clock was frustrating, but at least it ensured I was always ready for class. I would use the extra time provided by the early wake-up to review my lesson plans for the day. As I reviewed, I always felt very Chinese and very Peace Corps. I'd sip my *pu er* tea while listening to the singing. At about 7:30, I would head out for my daily *you tiao*. It was a Chinese breakfast, on top of Chinese tea and music. I would revel in my sense of immersion.

Despite eating fried dough for breakfast every morning and piles of greasy meats for lunch and dinner, I was actually losing weight. I felt healthier, in some ways, than I had in years. My diet in China may have been oil heavy but it was sugar and dairy free, a big change from the ice cream and pizza of Philadelphia. I was in love with Guizhou's spices, from *suan la jiao*, or "sour hot pepper," to *hua jiao*, a seed that I had never tasted in America and that numbed the tongue. I was eating everything from twice-fried pork to "red sauce porcupine." Each bite was delicious, though tinged with a bit of guilt for falling off the kosher wagon. If we are what we eat, then what was I becoming?

I felt daily pleasure from trying new food, daily guilt from eating forbidden animals, and daily bouts of queasiness brought on as I walked by Dog Meat King, an aptly named restaurant that was on the route from my apartment to my classroom. Its name—as well as the carcasses that dangled in its windows—made me pretty sure they weren't serving chicken. "That," I swore, "is one meat I'll *never* touch." My desire to immerse myself would only go so far.

◇

Campus was always quiet when I walked to class in the morning. I quickly acclimated to the chickens and stray dogs who greeted me. (I would shoo the dogs away from Dog Meat King, just to be safe.) I got used to the small groups of students scurrying to the bathhouse and the boys on the basketball court, who stopped their games just long enough to stare at me. Occasionally, I would join them for a few shots. No matter how many people were waiting for a spot on the court, they would always immediately add me to the game. I was finding the line between extreme graciousness and creepy curiosity difficult to identify. On the basketball court, behavior tended towards gracious, and the few minutes I would spend there always began and ended with handshakes and pats on the back.

The only creepy element developed a few weeks after my first time on the court. A man began appearing whenever I would play. He wore Nike warm-up gear and an old golf visor. He squatted in a grove of trees about twenty feet beyond the courts, smoking and watching me with narrowed eyes. He was wiry and athletic, and he was the only person I had seen in the city significantly taller than I was; he looked to be about six foot three. This Chinese giant would materialize whenever I stepped onto the court. He never said a word to me. He simply watched. It freaked me out, but I never had the nerve to approach him and ask what he was doing. He reminded me too much of Ivan Drago from *Rocky IV*.

In the afternoons after classes ended, when I headed home for *xiuxi*—the two-hour daily siesta that was deeply engrained into Guizhou culture—the campus seemed to stretch, take a deep breath, and relax. The only spot where people didn't slow down was the basketball court. At noon, the morning shoot-arounds transformed into hotly contested half-court games. First team to five points would win and stay on the court, and a good team would own it for an hour or more. Dozens of players watched each game, waiting for their turn and forgoing their nap time for a bit of exercise.

I could see the courts from the window in my office, and my walk home took me right past them. The regular ballers became accustomed to my schedule and waited courtside for me each day. At first, team captains who wanted me on their team were shy; they would delay their requests until I indicated I was ready to play. Once they realized I would play with whoever asked first, however, they engaged in a friendly arms race. The first to see me approach the court would run over and adopt me. After a few days of this, the entrepreneurial captains began creeping away from the courts around the time my classes ended in order to wait for me halfway up the road between the courts and my office. After a month, the captains waited for me at the front door of the Foreign Language Building. Eventually, some were bold enough to wait outside my classroom. They recruited me before I even had time to return my books to my office. This aggressiveness served them well in two ways: first, the captain who drafted me for the day could plant me under the basket where, treelike, I would raise my arms and wait for lob passes that were far above the outstretched hands of the diminutive undergraduates who could do nothing but gawk and cling to my torso. Second, it guaranteed that their team would not have to wait for a court. My team always had next.

Whenever I left the courts and continued my walk I would pass the occasional student using *xiuxi* as a time to practice recitation. These overachievers stood with open books in hand reading passages aloud in English and Chinese. At times, their recitations would come out as whispers, though some students on campus screamed according to the dictates of Crazy English, an organization headed by Li Yang, a teacher of enormous national fame. His followers—and there were millions of them—believed that Crazy English study methods guaranteed them improved scores in China's high-stakes national tests, the very tests President Bill had criticized in his drunken rant about the lack of creativity in Chinese students.

President Bill was certainly right about one thing: the entire Chinese education system was built on standardized tests. Each May, every single high school senior across the country sat for the *Gao Kao*, a kind of SAT on steroids. At around the same time, college seniors sat for the Chinese version of the LSAT, MCAT, GRE, and GMAT. Their scores on these tests were the sole methods for sorting them out as they moved on to the next stage of their academic career. A good score got them into a good program. A lousy score was ruinous.

The results of an educational system focused entirely on high-stakes tests were easy to see. Students spent six days a week, ten hours a day, from grades eight to twelve cramming information for the *Gao Kao*. They then spent college getting ready for the next round of tests. Anything that distracted students from figuring out how to fill in the blanks correctly was a waste of time. Sports and physical health were out. Music was out, as was sex ed. There were no glee clubs, school newspapers, yearbooks, or debate teams. All of this, along with other expressions of creativity, were mere distractions, as was critical thinking. Life for those who wanted to go to college (or on to grad school) was singularly focused on a number.

Li Yang, many people believed, could add a few precious points to this number. His Crazy English strategy was simple: yell while you learn, and yell at the top of your lungs. This, he believed, would increase confidence, an issue identified by many teachers as the number one problem for Chinese students. When Li travelled the country to give lectures, tens of thousands turned out to see him. He was something like a combination of L. Ron Hubbard, William J. McCorkle, and Howard

Gardner. He was also someone the Communist Party worried about; like Li Yuchun, the frighteningly popular winner of China's *Super Girl* competition, his power over young people made him seem a bit too Mao-like for anyone's comfort. "Li Yang is my hero!" Jackie screamed when I asked him why he always yelled when he spoke English. "My dream is to work for Crazy English! Nothing can stop my dream!"

The other educational businessman who had gotten rich by tapping into China's English craze was a Canadian named Mark Roswell. Chinese knew him as Da Shan, or Big Mountain. Big Mountain could be seen almost hourly on Chinese TV, in commercials shilling for his electronic dictionaries. In the commercials, he wore traditional kung fu clothing and spoke absolutely flawless Mandarin. Big Mountain set the standard for foreign speakers of Chinese; any time I spoke a complex, well-enunciated sentence, I could expect someone to tell me I was as good as Da Shan. I hated the bastard. In his commercials, students flocked to him and gushed with testimonials about how much his dictionary helped them learn. The camera always aimed up at him, and he was often framed by beams of light. The whole thing smacked of pop-fascism.

Both Li and Big Mountain were part of what I thought of as China's version of the Great Awakening. China's explosive Pentecostalism, however, was not focused on the Holy Ghost; it was focused on making a buck. If there was a midway point between the sensationalism of a Jonathan Edwards sermon from the 1700s ("There is nothing that keeps men out of hell but the mere pleasure of God") and a Wu-Tang Clan song from the 1990s ("C.R.E.A.M." [Cash Rules Everything Around Me]), it was a Big Mountain commercial.

After classes, swarms of students engaged in standing recitation with either Li Yang's books in their hands or Da Shan's dictionaries. Others would be sitting on newspapers they had strewn over rocks, looking over notes, or sending text messages.

There were also girls walking hand in hand, munching on ice-cream cones, and boys walking hand in hand towards the basketball courts.

Boy-girl combos were far less frequent than same-sex affection, a result of residual Maoism. The Chairman and his ardent followers believed romance was a bourgeois conceit, a form of what they called "spiritual pollution." Individual love, after all, distracted you from love of the Chairman and his party. From the mid-1960s until the mid-1980s, public displays of affection could get workers arrested and students expelled. Times, of course, change, and PDA had long been tolerated in China's coastal cities. Guizhou, however, with one foot still firmly planted in the Good Old Days, was not yet ready to dive into opposite-sex hand-holding. Still, I would on occasion turn a corner and catch a couple making out or, if they were really bold, groping each other. My presence would barely dissuade them.

"More and more of us want to be like Jack and Rose," Yvette told me when I asked about student romance. She was referring to the protagonists of *Titanic*, by far the most popular foreign film in Chinese history. It was the first Hollywood blockbuster played in Chinese cinemas after decades of total censorship, and its run in the theaters in the late 1990s was called the "*Titanic* Miracle." Jack and Rose became sirens of Western Love and their story a road map for young sentimentalists. The results were nauseating.

To wit: a few weeks into school, a sophomore stood outside the Foreign Language Building in the rain, wearing a cheap tuxedo and singing songs to his girlfriend who was in class on the second floor. The scene was straight out of *Say Anything*, except instead of John Cusack holding up a boom box playing "In Your Eyes," a malnourished Chinese teenager sang the ever-popular Carpenters hit, "Yesterday Once More," followed by an old favorite from Taiwanese star David Tao. The Tao song combined both

English and Chinese: "I love you *wu fa bu ai ni*, Baby *shuo ni ye ai wo*."

Not long after the serenade, another student stepped into love's ring of fire. He attempted to woo a girl by lining the hallway of the first floor of the Foreign Language Building with fake flower petals. The object of his affection came to my office to ask my advice. "Should I accept his love?" she asked me earnestly. She had a long nose, dark skin, bangs that ran straight along her eyebrows, and fingernails bitten to the cuticles. She wore a plaid skirt and a T-shirt with a kitten on it, which read "Romance Moment." I had no idea what to tell her.

Students often sought my advice on matters of the heart, since I came from the country that invented the Hollywood love story. I was the local Dan Savage. Questions about sex? Go to Mike's office. Wonder what to do with your boyfriend? Go to Mike's office. Want to know what looks hot? Go to Mike's office. "He has done such a romantic thing," said the girl with the flower-petaling suitor, "but I think he is ugly and short. What should I do?"

"Give the guy a chance," I said. "He really must like you."

She frowned and shook her head. "Life is easy for Americans. You've been falling in love since Shakespeare and have many examples to follow today. But Chinese do not know how to do it."

I pointed to her T-shirt. "What you need now," I assured her, "is a Romance Moment." This seemed to cheer her up, and she smiled.

"Even if his Romance Moment lasts only a minute, I will consider myself lucky!" she said while nodding.

I joined her affirmation. "You go, girl."

◇

Singing, flower petals, and sixty-second Romance Moments were nothing next to the romantic dénouement of the fall. In late October, Kitten (née Pussy) climbed to the top of her dormitory and threatened to jump off unless her ex-boyfriend got back together with her. Hundreds of students gathered at the foot of the building to take pictures, ogle, and participate in the power of Love. I feared for Kitten's well-being, but Shitty assured me it was just a show. "It is beautiful," she gushed as she looked up enviously at her apparently suicidal best friend. "She is like Juliet, waiting for her Romeo!"

"Yeah," I mumbled, "but Juliet kills herself in the end."

Shitty sighed breathlessly and nodded. "On our wonderful campus, this is romance."

Big Twin,
Little Twin

Between the basketball, the Crazy English, and the romance moments, I began to find campus a bit stuffy. A November heat wave didn't help: the temperature hovered around ninety degrees for most of the month. The boys at Gui Da eased their discomfort by walking around shirtless or, at the very least, attending class with their shirts rolled up above their nipples. They called it the "Guizhou air conditioner." If I imitated the practice I usually caused a bit of a stir. I have hair on my chest. Thick, Eastern European forests of hair. This example of biodiversity was unknown to Guizhou before my arrival and its introduction was deemed disgusting. "Wolf man," people would say as I walked by, just loud enough for me to hear. Or, "No wonder he's sweating. It is as if he is wearing a sweater."

I could usually laugh to myself at these comments, though they contributed to my desire to broaden my horizons and get off campus. To this end, I started taking long walks along the river across the street from my apartment. As my confidence grew, my walks lengthened. I took advantage of the weather on one blessedly cool afternoon and followed the river for more than an hour. I wandered in and out of a handful of villages, each made up of a dozen or so houses. I was heading north, away from Huaxi and towards central Guiyang, meandering wherever my curiosity took me. A breeze blew down from the mountains to my right. Traffic from the highway crawled along to my left. I was happy to be out on the dirt paths exploring life beyond the confines of Gui Da.

As the sun dipped towards the top of the mountains, I bought a watermelon slice from a roadside vendor. I was at the outskirts of a village quite a bit larger than the others I had passed. This was, in fact, one of the villages Dean Wang had pointed out to me on my first day in Guiyang as we drove from the train station to Gui Da. "You won't like that place," he had told me. "It's not safe." It was time to find out if the dean was right.

I thanked the watermelon seller and left the path along the river, veering onto a smaller path that headed east towards the mountains. An archway marking the entrance to the village was only a few hundred yards ahead. It was on the far side of a small bridge leading over a tributary of the river. A few fishermen leaned over the sides of the bridge, carefully casting their lines to avoid a huddle of women washing dishes along the riverbed. As the sounds of the highway faded away completely, I passed under the archway. Pasted inside were yellowed propaganda posters. "Family Planning Helps Strengthen the People," read the largest poster. It was accompanied by a phrase from a famous 1973 campaign, *wan xi shao*, or "Later, Sparser, Fewer." Most of the platitudes directed at the village seemed to be about reducing population.

There was also a brand-new poster listing President Hu Jintao's *Ba Rong Ba Chi*, or "eight Honors and eight Dishonors," a vague and often-mocked list of political platitudes:

LOVE THE COUNTRY; DO IT NO HARM.

SERVE THE PEOPLE; NEVER BETRAY THEM.

FOLLOW SCIENCE; DISCARD SUPERSTITION.

BE DILIGENT; NOT INDOLENT.

BE UNITED, HELP EACH OTHER; MAKE NO GAINS AT OTHERS'
EXPENSE.

BE HONEST AND TRUSTWORTHY; DO NOT SACRIFICE ETHICS
FOR PROFIT.

BE DISCIPLINED AND LAW-ABIDING; NOT CHAOTIC AND
LAWLESS.

LIVE PLAINLY, WORK HARD; DO NOT WALLOW IN LUXURIES
AND PLEASURES.

Hu Jintao promoted these propaganda couplets in a huge
national blitz. *Ba Rong Ba Chi* posters eventually went up at rail-
road stations, schools, and village entrances across China. My
students memorized them and chanted them when Gui Da was
inspected by provincial officials. In private, however, they called
the campaign the "eight borings, and eight sillies." I hadn't met
anyone who took them very seriously.

I passed under the archway and entered the village. I found
a maze of tightly packed houses, crumbling streets, and corru-
gated metal. The older houses were made of piled rocks and
recycled wood; the newer houses were made of cement and pink
bathroom tile. The air smelled of grass, body odor, and wet
cement. Ducks, scrawny dogs, and children took one look at me
and ran off. The streets were covered in a veritable cornucopia
of shit—bird, pig, cow, human, and unknown.

As I continued to walk, I noticed a few of the village kids
beginning to follow me. By the time I had walked the village
from end to end and passed out the rear gate—a slow stroll that
had taken no more than ten minutes—there were half a dozen
children in my wake. They seemed to range in age from about

six to ten. There were four girls and two boys staying close to each other and maintaining a careful fifteen-yard buffer zone between their gaggle and my lead. If I slowed down, they slowed down. If I sped up, they kept pace. I was walking on a path strewn with broken bricks, past the northern edge of the village. To my left and right were fields of sorghum and cabbage. Far ahead, I could see a train tunnel leading into a mountain. After walking a bit farther I stopped and turned around. The children began giggling uncontrollably. They looked at me wide-eyed.

"Hello," I said, smiling.

The kids immediately screamed and ran for cover in the trees. I stood for a few moments, amused, before turning and continuing my walk. They crept back out of the trees and began following again. I listened to their whispering and snickering. The sounds reminded me of visits to my younger brother's home in Denmark, where the laughter of his son and daughter is the most joyful sound I can imagine.

I walked for a few more minutes before sitting in the shade under a stunted tree. The gaggle didn't seem to know how to react. At first they just stood in the road. Eventually, the two boys got bored and walked back towards the village. The girls decided to stay and began playing with Pokémon cards. They would occasionally glance over at me, but I was soon part of the background. I was able to observe their game out of the corners of my eyes. They were laying the cards on the path and slapping at them, trying to use the wind generated from the movement of their hands to flip the cards from front to back. A successful flip seemed to mean you could keep the card.

The four girls looked similar. Sisters, I wondered? Eventually I made eye contact with the girl who seemed to be the leader of the troop.

"Little sister," I said using the polite greeting for a stranger her age, "how old are you?" I was speaking the clearest Mandarin I could muster. The game of Pokémon came to a sudden halt.

"I'm fourteen," she told me, standing up straight. She had a red bandana tied around her neck and wore black track pants with a white T-shirt reading "We find a piece of soil." The T-shirt included a picture of a mug of coffee shedding a tear. The other three girls continued squatting over their cards though they did not restart the game. They were listening carefully, but working on nonchalance.

"Are all of you sisters?" I asked.

The leader smiled and dropped a single word of English: "No." She went back to Chinese: "These two are my sisters." She pointed at the youngest girls, both of whom were wearing matching three-quarter-length jeans and light-yellow T-shirts. As I looked at them directly, I realized their clothing wasn't all that matched: they were twins. The leader continued with the introductions, pointing to the fourth girl. "She is our cousin." The cousin, unlike the twins, took the risk of smiling at me. She also offered a halting wave and a sudden blush.

"How old are they?" I asked.

"My sisters are eleven, and my cousin is fourteen, like me."

As usual in China, my attempt to guess age had failed completely. The twins looked like they were about seven years old, and cousin and leader looked not a day over ten. "How old do you think I am?" I asked.

"You are nineteen."

It was my turn to laugh. "No, I am twenty-nine. I was born in the Year of the Dragon."

The girls were astonished. They stopped their game and tentatively approached the tree I was still leaning against. The twins started climbing it. Leader stood over me. Cousin sat down next to me and looked at the hair on my arm.

"You're very hairy," she told me.

"I know. I'm a wolf man."

The girls laughed hysterically at this, and I joined them. I had fled campus hoping to get away from comments about my differences, but a group of giggling middle schoolers felt irresistibly endearing. As a general rule, kids get a free pass with me—except for frog-stomping kids—and I found the girls particularly adorable. I was enjoying our banter. The opportunity to poke fun at myself actually made me feel light-hearted.

One of the twins was laughing from a perch above me in the tree, and I worried she would fall out. "Be careful," I told her, which prompted her to dangle upside down, hanging precariously with her legs. I shrugged my shoulders and decided it would be best if I, too, climbed the tree. From the reaction of the girls, this was definitely the first time any of them had seen a grown wolf man participating in their games. I climbed for all I was worth and soon managed to get myself stuck about fifteen feet off the ground. "I don't think I can move," I told one of the twins as I clung desperately to a bending branch.

"I will help you," she said, shaking her head. She scampered to the branch below me and guided my feet to a series of secure nubs. It took a few minutes, but I finally made it back to flat ground.

"America is a developed country," the other twin said to me from far above, "but China has better tree climbers."

◈

I played a few games with the girls that afternoon, from Poké-mon to hopscotch, and after about an hour, as darkness settled, we started walking back to the village. With their shyness now fully behind them they became a talkative bunch. They told me they were part of the Wang family, as was just about everyone in the village. The twins, who were apparently named Big Twin and Little Twin, and their older sister—who told me to call her

Wang Number One—lived in a house at the foot of the mountains. Their father was a leader in the village. Cousin Wang lived not far away. Her father was a cop in Guiyang.

The girls also told me they were Bouyei, as Dean Wang had led me to expect. The Bouyei were an ethnic minority group totaling no more than three million people. They had been in Guizhou more than a thousand years and had always been fiercely independent. The emperors used to refer to them as the "barbarians of the west." Prejudices about them remained strong in the minds of Han Chinese.

"He cannot learn because he is a minority," Jackie told me during our first class, referring to Gordon. Dean Wang called the Bouyei "primitive." Unsurprisingly, Jackie and the dean were wrong. Gordon may have introduced himself as "Moron," but he was one of my fastest learners. The Wang girls were smart, funny, and tuned in to American culture. As we played Pokémon, they led me in a fairly kick-ass rendition of *NSYNC's "Bye Bye Bye," complete with MTV-style dance moves. They also asked me some impressive questions. Cousin Wang: "Are there any Bouyei in your United States?" Big Twin: "How old are the girls when they get married in America?" Wang Number One: "Does your country still have slavery?" These questions displayed more curiosity than the usual, "Can you use our Chinese chopsticks?" I felt like this group of little girls was more honest and open than many of the adults I had met at Gui Da. I decided that next time I saw Dean Wang I'd ask him to explain why he thought the Bouyei were primitive. I also decided I would be more confrontational next time one of my Han students said something I perceived as racist. I was nervous to do so: identity politics clearly had a different context in China. I would nevertheless try something more direct than asking questions or sputtering out niceties. I was tired of being such a PC PCV and relying on polite passivity.

When we reached the gate of the village, I told the girls I had to head home. "Will you visit us again?" asked Wang Number One.

"I'll be back at the same time next week," I promised. The girls smiled, waved, and headed into the village. I returned to campus with a new perspective, happier than I'd been in weeks.

—┼—

Walmart

After the November heat wave, the weather began to cool. It was a welcome reprieve, though I was soon grumbling just as much about the cold as I had about the heat. The temperature never dipped below fifty degrees, but with no indoor heating anywhere on campus, it always felt chilly. I started teaching in a jacket, scarf, and hat. The leaves began turning yellow and dropping off the trees. Rain fell each afternoon, and I never left home without my umbrella.

Despite the foul weather, classes were going well. Best of all, the Guj had turned out far better than I expected. During the four or five meetings we had held, we cooked challah, matzah-ball soup, and other Jewish foods. Our mission soon expanded: Jennifer asked if we could make pizza. "I love the idea," I responded, "but we would need to find someone selling cheese." I already had an oven (one of the few in the city, purchased from a Canadian missionary). I had olive oil (purchased at the Guiyang Walmart, though the 25-fluid-ounce bottle cost me a full day's salary). Flour, yeast, and vegetables were no problem. As for cheese? I had never seen it served in restaurants in Guiyang or sold in stores.

"There must be a way to find the cheese," Jennifer said. "After all, our city has a Pizza Hut."

She had a point. In the late 1990s, Yum! Brands foods had come to town. By 2005, the city had three KFCs and, as a flagship eating establishment, a Pizza Hut. It was one of the hottest restaurants in town, a place where businessmen brought top clients and students went on fancy dates. I had no real hope of eating there: international Peace Corps policy is to pay volunteers a stipend that lets them live at a level commensurate with those in their communities. In China, this meant about $125 each month. PCVs took buses not taxis, overnight trains not planes, and ate noodles not pizza. Pizza Hut charged American prices. A ten-dollar dinner was out of the question. Jennifer expanded her chest and got a determined look on her face. "I will find us the cheese."

For two days, Jennifer worked her *guanxi* and sent me almost hourly text message updates on her progress. *Walmart has slices of American cheese will it work?* This was followed by *Local hotels have no cheese one has mayonnaise will this work?* Finally, I received a message that was more hopeful: *restaurant supply store has cheese must investigate.* I waited to hear more.

When Jennifer caught up with me later that day, she was giddy. "This really might work," she told me. "But you must come with me to buy the cheese so that we are sure it is authentic. I do not want to get cheated." We set a day for a cheese hunt and informed the Guj that our next meeting would include pizza. Everyone was excited, but no one more so than Jennifer's roommate, Vivian. She had been increasing her level of Guj involvement week by week. Her interest in Judaism was actually getting a little bit overwhelming for me. "Jewish learning makes me happy," she had said at the last meeting. Challah, prayers over wine, and Woody Allen movies were drawing her out of her shell.

Was I becoming a missionary? The Guj was starting to

make me feel twinges of Peace Corps guilt. As the feeling grew, however, so did the insights the club helped me gain into life in Guizhou. Teacher Qing's life in Chengdu could have been the stuff of a *Wall Street Journal* profile: she was educated, Western-ized, nonideological, and profit driven. She was Thomas Fried-man's kind of Chinese, happy that Opening and Reform had given her access to Chanel handbags, high-rise living, and English lessons. Vivian, on the other hand, was not so happy that the world was flat. Her life was undeniably improving, yet she had a painful feeling of falling farther and farther behind. She wasn't quite sure what she was falling behind. Was it the West? Was it women in Beijing and Chengdu? Was it Korea and Japan? The vague nature of her pain made it even more difficult for her to bear.

"I am drifting," Vivian once told me. "All of China is drifting." Without religion, without honest history, without tradition, without even an open possibility of motherhood (thanks to the One Child Policy), she felt unmoored. When she looked in my Chinese-English dictionary for the perfect word to describe her feelings, she chose "ennui." Life in Chengdu or on the Chinese coast offered career and money as guiding principles. But in Guiyang, these pursuits struck locals the way a career in jazz dance would strike the average Kansan. What was the point, and who were the role models? Vivian was unsure where to turn for advice. The Guj gave her temporary hope.

◇

Jennifer and I headed out for the restaurant-supply store after classes on a cool November afternoon and within an hour we were at the edge of the People's Park at the heart of the city. We were also at the entrance to the Walmart.

The Walmart was, in some ways, the perfect physical mani-festation of Guiyang's personality. It was housed in a forty-thousand-square-foot warehouse submerged beneath the People's

Park, a public square constructed at Mao's behest in the center of the city. The People's Park was a downsized version of an even larger public space, Tiananmen Square in Beijing (the largest pedestrian mall in the world, and a space Mao had hoped would be large enough to hold one billion people). Both squares served a similar purpose: they were to be the gathering place for the celebration of the victory of the proletariat over the forces of global capitalism.

In the late 1960s, Guiyang peasants were required to join hands in the People's Park, face the thirty-foot-tall statue of the Chairman that towered on its eastern edge, and sing songs like "Workers, Peasants and Army, Unite!" The words of the song were engraved on a plaque near the statue:

> Workers, peasants and army march forward, millions with one heart
> Wipe out the enemy, the capitalists, imperialists, and reactionaries
> Workers, peasants and army march, the final victory is ours!

That was then. In 2005, by contrast, Guiyang residents eased past the granite visage of the Chairman and made their way towards a replica of the Louvre Pyramid built in the center of the park in the late 1990s. The pyramid housed an escalator that (when actually running) whisked shoppers down into the bowels of the capitalist mother ship. The statue of Mao, a slight smile on his lips, appeared to be offering a friendly greeting to the yellow Walmart smiley face painted on the Louvre Pyramid. The two icons stood less than fifty yards apart. The smiley face looked directly into the Chairman's groin.

"Do you think it is strange that your city has a Walmart next to a statue of Chairman Mao?" I asked Jennifer as we walked by the park.

She thought about this for a moment. "I think this statue is too big," was her cryptic response. We looked up. The Chairman's hand was the size of my torso. The pedestal on which he stood put his feet at my eye level. They looked like piano benches.

"He is pretty big," I agreed.

"It is good to remember our Chairman," Jennifer continued, "but it is better to develop. Walmart is the future, and Chairman Mao is the past." Jennifer frowned and quickened her pace. We walked in silence for a few moments before she began speaking again, this time with frustration in her voice. "His statue should be smaller. To be honest, I hate Chairman Mao. What can he help me do?" She paused, looked back over her shoulder at the statue, and snorted. "Can he find me a husband? A better job? Of course not."

Jennifer looked like she had a lot more to say about Mao and the Walmart, so I stood and waited patiently. She started speaking and stopped again three or four times before eventually diving into a story about Walmart, love, and life among the other billion.

"When I first began teaching at Gui Da, I was extremely lonely. Most men do not want to marry someone as short as me, so I often felt depressed. The only thing that matters to young Chinese nowadays is looking sexy and having money. I am too fat, so at first I tried dieting, but I still could not find a husband. I went to the diet clinic every day and even started fainting. It was a famous diet clinic, but it did not work. It was at that time that I determined to become rich. If I cannot have a husband, at least I can have a car and an apartment! I started going to the Walmart every day for inspiration. I would walk the aisles for hours. Sometimes I would pretend my Prince Charming was just around the corner and would soon find me, but I knew it would never happen. Actually, I don't even want a Prince Charming or a Jack and Rose story. I just want a man who is honest and works hard. If I find him in the Walmart, I know we will be compatible because he and I both want things that are the best."

Jennifer was looking past me as she spoke. I wasn't sure if she was staring at the Louvre Pyramid or the Chairman. I found her honesty moving and her self-awareness bowled me over. Still, I felt confused. Was Jennifer a confident woman navigating with aplomb the choppy waters of a changing China? Or was she rudderless and adrift?

She concluded her story. "Recently, I have begun to hate Walmart. I realize that just as Chairman Mao cannot inspire me or teach me, neither can capitalism. There is no value in anything." Her gaze returned from the middle distance and focused on me for a moment. She bit her bottom lip, spun on her heels, and continued walking.

十二

Parmesan Cheese

We walked past the Mao statue. We walked past salesmen hocking pirated DVDs. We walked past stalls selling dumplings stuffed with red-bean paste and others selling cheap clothing. We paused, briefly, to buy a plastic cup full of *chou doufu*, a bit of street food that lived up to its literal translation, "stinky tofu." Along with dog meat, the dish was one of the few in Guiyang that I simply could not eat. It stank of rotting, fermented vegetables. I imagined a zombie's breath would smell similar and I gagged whenever I tried eating it. Jennifer wolfed it down by the fistful.

The streets were as bustling as ever, and I was getting my usual stares as well as the occasional "Hello!" After about fifteen minutes, we turned into a side alley and entered a busy marketplace. A hundred-yard-long tunnel with tables on both sides and a plastic tarp running high above, it was one of dozens of outdoor markets in Guiyang. The smaller markets had stalls selling vegetables brought in fresh from the countryside, dozens of kinds of soy products, as well as meat and eggs. Large markets were bazaars of electronics, knickknacks, and car parts. This one was only midsized, though the tarp trapped and concentrated the noise of the customers and salespeople, making it feel much larger. I was reminded of Mos Eisley, the city where Luke Skywalker first met Han Solo.

As we entered the tunnel we saw spice sellers (star anise, cinnamon, nutmeg, dried peppers), vegetable stands (eggplant, tomato, ginger, cabbage), and piles of fresh watermelons, mangos, and apples. About fifteen yards into the tunnel, we hit the meat stands. The meat was piled high in an impressive array of shapes and colors. There were live animals as well, most of them moments away from slaughter. "Fresh meat costs more," Jennifer told me as she hustled through the tunnel. I looked at the prices: newly slaughtered chicken was about a dollar a pound; "old chicken," a handwritten advertisement announced, was "open to negotiation."

There were a few people haggling over mounds of beef, and a few more laying down money and selecting the birds, mammals, and aquatic life they wanted freshly slaughtered. Blood flowed in the alley, in places an inch deep. The market smelled bad. Real bad. The tarp was trapping more than noise: it was also capturing the fragrance of sweating, unwashed people, slowly rotting food, and death. I was feeling a little queasy, so I went over to a spice dealer hoping the smell of the cinnamon would help me feel better. There were piles of mahogany-colored beans, bright-yellow powders, and dark-brown nuts. I focused on breathing slowly, and my stomach began to calm. Within a few beats, I was ready to catch up to Jennifer.

When I looked to my right to find her, I was surprised to see the body of a skinned dog dangling from a metal hook pushed through its mouth. It looked like a Chihuahua. Beneath this carcass was the rear half of a beagle lying on a cutting board. A tiny middle-aged woman with teeth set at ninety-degree angles stood behind the dogs, with a huge smile on her face. She looked directly in my eyes and laughed maniacally.

Kaleidoscope vision set in, and I suddenly felt like I was at a

Sam Raimi *Army of Darkness* carnival. I bounded away from the dog meat, nausea returning. The farther I walked, the more surreal the carnival around me became. Hundreds of live chickens; fish tanks full of both live and dead squid and octopus; duck heads, feet, and gizzards; deep-fried maggots on sticks; unidentified, purplish meat piled five feet high on tables; children pointing at me and screaming "Hello!"

And finally, the end of the tunnel.

Jennifer grabbed me by the wrist and pulled me out of the nightmare. She gave me a stern look while pointing towards a store at the end of the block. "There is the cheese."

We resumed our brisk pace and soon stood before a kitchen-supply store. There were pots, pans, and woks hanging in the windows. I was breathing heavily, trying not to vomit. "Americans do not eat dog meat," Jennifer told me. She was looking less and less stern, and more and more concerned by my ashen face. I sat on the edge of the curb and put my head in my hands. "In China, only the Buddhists avoid meat, but we think of them as superstitious." Was she trying to comfort me? I remained silent, so Jennifer continued. "There is a joke: Chinese people eat everything with four legs except the table, and in Guangdong, even the table isn't safe." I winced, looking up at Jennifer. "I know it's not such a good joke," she said. "And I know dog meat is unusual for you, but now that you are in China, you have a chance to try it."

I could finally respond without puking: "I'll think about it," I lied.

"You do not have to worry about the quality of the meat. We can buy it in Walmart."

I was taken aback. "Walmart sells dog meat?"

"Yes," replied Jennifer, reaching out a hand to help me up off the curb. I stood unsteadily. "And the price is always low. It is always the lowest. Walmart has the best prices in our city."

I shook my head in disbelief. It was odd enough to think of

a dead-dog section of a Walmart, but what was even more unbelievable was that they could undercut the prices of butchers in outdoor markets, who were squeezing out a subsistence living.

"Aren't you worried about that?" I asked Jennifer as we began walking. "I mean, if Walmart wipes out all these other marketplaces, what will happen to the people who work here?"

Jennifer turned her head to the side quizzically. "It is simply competition, Mike. It is the new way in China. I thought all Americans would understand this." Jennifer suddenly took a quick breath. "Oh, I just thought of something! The Walmart might even have kosher dog meat! We could eat it for our next Guj!"

As I pondered the permeability of Jennifer's cultural membrane, we prepared to enter the kitchen-supply store. Before doing so, the adjacent record store started blasting Li Yuchun's "Sweetheart, I Love You." Jennifer and I reflexively began singing along. We laughed together, temporarily forgetting about kosher dog meat.

"I like this song," I told her. She nodded, and we continued to sing. We also sang along to the next tune that blasted from the speakers, "God is a Girl," one of China's biggest foreign hits. The song was originally performed by Groove Coverage, a Berlin-based acid-elevator music band. It was popularized in China by a Singaporean-Chinese singer called Guo Mei Mei. "God is a girl," the lyrics began, before asking a couple of questions: "Do you believe it? Can you receive it?"

Guo Mei Mei had a couple of other hits as well, all of which were controversial. She had no original music. Instead, everything was a cover. She had made a techno version of the Chinese folk song, "I Love You Like a Mouse Loves Rice" and had become a superstar with a song she called "Bu Pa Bu Pa," a rip-off of a Moldovan pop hit from the band O-Zone. To some, this typified China's inability to innovate. "She is too fake," Jennifer once told me. "China must stop imitating and begin to create

on its own." I was sure President Bill would agree. To me, however, Guo Mei Mei was a symbol of the new China, combining
cultures, languages, fashions, and pop-cues from around the
world. Her music wasn't half bad.

We listened to the music until my stomach was completely
settled and then entered the restaurant-supply store. Towards
the back, tucked in the corner, was a freezer. Inside the freezer
were bricks of long-frozen cheese. I pulled out a two-foot-long,
twenty-five-pound log of frozen parmesan, feeling like Oliver
Twist. It would be enough cheese for a year. "Now you can cook
us pizza for Shabbat!" Jennifer was twitching with excitement.

"This is great!" I said, patting her on the back. She blushed,
and smiled. We had a brief argument about who would pay for
the cheese, eventually agreeing to split the cost. We hustled back
to the bus, hoping to make it home to Gui Da before rush hour.

◇

Pizza night went off without a hitch. Jennifer was able to bask in
a bit of glory for having organized the party; Vivian—stuffed
full of dairy—was more talkative than I had ever seen her; the
half-dozen regulars who joined us were relaxed and happy. There
were also two first-time visitors to the club: a computer science
major whom I had never met, and Kevin Chen, the People's Liberation Army poster boy and class monitor.

The computer science major was short, stout, and, like Jackie,
a devotee of Crazy English. "Hello Mike it is nice to meet you
I am Shamus I am here to practice my English with you!" he
yelled breathlessly after entering the apartment. I asked him to
stop yelling which, from the look on his face, seemed a bit like
asking a six-year-old to stop loving ice cream. He quieted down
but never drifted more than a few feet from my elbow. The only
moment when he returned to unpunctuated sentences spoken at
concert-level volume was when Dean Wang came up in discussion. In passing, Vivian mentioned that Dean Wang had retired

a few years ago but been dragged back to work by his *danwei*. "It is true!" Shamus blurted, as if I doubted the veracity of Vivian's statement. "Dean Wang is famous in our university. We cannot afford to lose him!"

"You mean he can't quit?" I asked, half to Vivian and half to Shamus. I imitated the Godfather. "Every time I think I'm out, they pull me back *in*."

"He must serve his country," Shamus responded, ignoring my attempt at channeling Michael Corleone. Vivian clicked her tongue at Shamus and rolled her eyes.

This led to a longer discussion about retirement. Jennifer told me that the retirement age in Guizhou was fifty-five for women and sixty for men. "This is because men are stronger and therefore prefer to work longer," Shamus explained to me. I asked Vivian how retirees made ends meet. Shamus again: "Our government takes care of all of us."

"They *used* to take care of all of us," Jennifer corrected, her voice coming to us from the kitchen, where she was putting a batch of pizza in the small oven I had carried over from my apartment. It was slightly larger than an Easy-Bake child's toy, so our pizzas were no larger than CDs. Jennifer continued: "We are all on our own now."

Nods from most of the people in room. Shamus, however, was displeased. "It is true that we must struggle more now that we have given back the iron rice bowl," he said with a frown, "but China still takes care of us." I noticed that Shamus had a bit of a Scottish accent along with his Scottish name. He had probably picked up both from whatever foreign teacher (or missionary) he had first met. He quieted down to a conspiratorial whisper. "Science can also take care of us. The British have invented a pill that will let you live with great health for 150 years." Vivian rolled her eyes again, this time with an audible sigh. The other students, however, seemed intrigued. Yvette even exclaimed, "How wonderful!"

"But," Shamus continued ominously, leaning forward in his chair, "the Americans are not allowing the British to sell the pill because Americans hate old people and do not want to pay for their retirement."

Many eyes turned towards me. The image of the greedy, selfish American had been around in China for a long time. Mao built the most impressive scaffolding for this image during the Korean War, or, as it was known in China, the "Aid Korea, Resist America" campaign. Like many skilled politicians, Mao was a master at creating an Other against which he could tilt. He riled his people into a Communist, jingoist froth, imploring them to rally to his side in defense against capitalist aggression. America became an Imperialist Dog and a Paper Tiger. To me, these sound like cool names for Brooklyn hipster bands. To Chinese in the 1950s, however, they were rallying cries for battle, self-sacrifice, and confidence in the future victory of the Communist system. Mao was so invested in the Korean conflict and in stopping an American incursion at his eastern border that he sent his own son to the front lines. Mao Jr. died in Korea along with more than a million other Chinese.

Korea is the "forgotten war" for Americans, but it was burned sharply into the minds of all of my students, colleagues, and friends. Mao had tapped into something real: the terror of having the world's most powerful nation knocking at the door with tanks, and knocking only a few years after China finally ended decades of war, civil strife, and subjugation at foreign hands. Seeing the Korean War from the Chinese perspective was depressing. It made America look like a raving, angry, arrogant monster. Mao was only too happy to have this convenient enemy around to help him justify his excesses. "America dropped an atomic bomb on Japan," Yvette once told me, "sent its army to Korea, invaded Vietnam, sent the CIA to Tibet, bombed Cambodia, built bases in Okinawa, and stationed its navy around Taiwan. At a time when we were weak and you were very strong, you surrounded us with violence. This is what we remember."

Ugh.

Shamus had internalized this and more. I knew I ought to be sensitive, but my instinctual response to his statement that America hated the elderly was to push things to the absurd. "Yeah, I hate old people," I considered saying, "but you know who really pisses me off? Jews. And babies. And unicorns. They're all a bunch of assholes."

Sarcasm, I knew, would be lost in translation. Confrontation would have been hugely problematic as well. But I had promised myself to go beyond polite passivity. I decided to go with a question: "Where did you hear this news?"

"I read it in a book," Shamus told us.

I looked around to try to get a sense of what others in the group were thinking. Eyebrows were raised but I had no idea if this was a warning or mere curiosity. I went with this: "In America, not all books are true. Are all books true in China?" I asked the question as pointedly as I could.

"Yes," said Shamus. "I believe them."

I nodded. What was the next step? What were Shamus's intentions? Was he picking a fight? Did he hope I would correct him? Who was he? Was he someone I needed to "respect" (meaning, in my impression of Chinese etiquette, defer to and obey)? Was he being culturally insensitive? Was he trying, in some way, to treat me the way he thought Americans wanted to be treated? My quick conclusion was that he had been so pickled in the misinformation that made up "news" in Guiyang that he was not even to blame. Still, there was an ocean of cultural confusion in our brief interaction: perceptions of media and truth; power dynamics based on age; language barriers. There were social cues I knew I was missing. There were definitions of professionalism and collegiality of which I felt sharply unaware.

"Shamus," I finally said after a long silence, "if I tell you that this pill does not exist, will you believe me or your book?"

He blinked at me and did not respond. Before we could continue, Jennifer cried out from the kitchen, "Pizza is ready!" Everyone jumped to their feet and scurried off to grab a slice.

◇

Kevin showed up a few minutes later. No one in the room seemed very happy to see him. His classmates steered clear of him for most of the evening. He was, as usual, polite, formal, and soft-spoken. He clearly noticed that the other students were avoiding him, but he never appeared upset or frustrated. Instead, he seemed to be working hard to put them at ease. He laughed at everyone's jokes (even the bad ones), and he made sure he was the last one to take a slice of pizza. He also stayed after the party to help wash dishes.

"Did you have fun tonight?" I asked him as he dried the plates Jennifer was rinsing.

"I enjoyed the pizza," he replied simply.

"It seems," I said slowly, "like some of the other students were surprised to see you here." I was attempting to be tactful. My real sentiment was closer to *why does everyone treat you like a leper?*

Vivian chortled at my statement. Her cheese-induced high had her more extroverted than I had ever seen her. "They were not happy to see Kevin because he is their class monitor," she said without looking up from the sink.

"I'm still a little unclear on that," I admitted. "What exactly is a 'monitor'?"

Kevin waited to see if Vivian would answer the question. When she did not, he stopped drying the dishes for a moment and looked up at the ceiling. "The monitor has a very important job," he told me. "We are chosen to make sure there is order in the class." Kevin went on to explain that in every classroom in

China, from first grade through graduate school, students nominated a slate of candidates from which the teachers selected a monitor. The teachers usually chose the tallest male (which was how Kevin got his job). Some monitors dodged their responsibilities until they were replaced. Others, like Kevin, took the job seriously. He would rouse from bed the students who were chronic late sleepers; he would raise money for others who needed to go to the hospital; he would levy fines if students misbehaved or failed tests, organize outings to Huaxi park, and meet with teachers who were displeased with the class's performance. His description made the monitor seem like some sort of bouncer-nanny hybrid.

"That's a lot of responsibility," I told him when he finished his summary.

"Yes," Vivian added, "and Kevin takes it too seriously. The teachers have all told him these old jobs don't matter anymore, but he is too traditional. So his classmates hate him."

My Chinese friends used the term "hate" liberally, but I still cringed. Kevin simply shrugged. "I enjoy the job," he told us. "At least it gives me some things to do. Without it, the life of the student would be meaningless to me."

Kevin finished drying the dishes in silence. At the end of the evening, he shook my hand, thanked me for the pizza, and walked out alone.

十三

All Foreigners
Are Bastards

There was a downside to pizza night. The taste of melted, greasy cheese awoke in me a strong desire for comfort food. I started dreaming of eggplant parm and lox and bagels. I also had a strange yearning for matzah; Passover, after all, was just around the corner. I e-mailed my mom and asked her to mail me a box of matzah meal so I could cook up some holiday food. It would take a month to arrive by slow boat.

In the meantime, my best option for a taste from my childhood was KFC. I hadn't been to a fast-food joint in years, but the Happy Meal was a fixture of my childhood. My grandparents were huge fans of hamburgers, and even bigger fans of the senior-citizen discount. They took me on regular trips to McDonald's, Wendy's, and—on special occasions—Arby's. The first time I fell in love, it was with an order of Arby's curly fries. Our affair lasted from second to sixth grade. Alyssa Milano—child star of the 1980s sitcom *Who's the Boss?*—then supplanted the heavily seasoned fries as the primary object of my desires.

My tastes changed as I got older, but the idea of a bucket of fried chicken, a paper cup full of Coke, and a side of fries grew more and more appealing as I ate bowl after bowl of rice. I found myself yearning for an injection of salt and high-fructose corn syrup. I decided to make a trip into the center of Guiyang to satisfy my urge.

◇

The newest of Guiyang's KFCs was attached to Beijing Hualian, a Chinese-owned chain of supermarkets working hard to compete with Walmart. Local yuppies endlessly debated the pros and cons of the two businesses. The Hualian crowd wanted to support a Chinese-owned company; the Walmart crowd thought of everything Chinese as inferior. Hualian shoppers could earn the cachet of the local. Walking around town with a Walmart shopping bag, on the other hand, gave the Guiyang yuppie a patina of globalization. I found the stores largely identical, especially since both housed a KFC. The Hualian was a bit closer to campus, so it was there that I would get my fast-food fix.

For weeks, I saved a small bit of my Peace Corps stipend, building up a slush fund. When my kitty was full, I headed to the bus stop. I waited for the 109, which would take me to the center of town. It appeared after only a few minutes, and the doorman leaned out and waved at me as the bus slowed and approached the curb. I ran alongside the bus and he pulled me aboard, holding onto my arm until I was safely seated near the front of the bus. I paid my two yuan and watched the river race by as we bombed down the highway.

Most of the seats on Chinese buses were too small for me, though if I lucked out and ended up on a bench near the door I could actually lounge in relative comfort. I had one such seat on that day and stretched out. I was happy to feel the cold air blowing through the open windows. I was happy there were no smokers on board the bus. I was happy we didn't hit much traffic. I flipped open my copy of *The Lord of the Rings*. Frodo was at the black gates of Barad-dûr, a city I was sure had toilets even worse than Guiyang.

I was jerked out of the novel as the bus swerved to the side of the road so the doorman could drag aboard two middle-aged men in leather jackets. I noticed that the first had a small white dog in his hands. It looked like a shih tzu. The second man had a half-full pillowcase. The man with the dog sat two seats to my right. The man with the pillowcase sat next to me. Out of the corner of my eye, I noticed that the pillowcase—just threadbare enough to see through—was full of puppies. The man was holding the pillowcase tightly around the puppies, and I worried they would have trouble breathing. I closed my book and collected the appropriate vocabulary in my head. I didn't want to repeat another frog-stomping incident, but I wanted to intervene.

As the two men began a conversation, the puppies started squirming around, probably trying to find a way to get enough air. The man with the sack closed the fist of his free hand, wound back, and punched the bag of dogs. One of the dogs let out the sound of a lung being crushed. It stopped moving. The other puppies continued to squirm, so the man continued to pound away at them.

I was paralyzed. I had gotten over the shock of some mistreatment of animals. I had students who would carry new kittens around in plastic trash bags. I had seen people dragging dogs behind them on chains. I had walked in rivers of animal blood. But this man's treatment of the puppies seemed beyond the laissez-faire freedom afforded China's animal abusers. Still, no one else on the bus batted an eye.

Perhaps punching a dog was the Chinese moral equivalent of whipping a mule?

No. Clearly what I was seeing was wrong. Clearly this was not a situation where I just needed to ride the cultural wave or integrate into foreign culture. The others on the bus, I assumed, were as disgusted as I was but were not able to stop the man because they were constrained by concepts of saving face. I was not constrained. No more Peace Corps tolerance. No more Mr. Nice Guy. It was time to embrace my inner Ugly American.

I turned to the man and asked him what he was doing. He stopped punching and stared at me. I asked again. He laughed, elbowed his friend, and said, "The foreigner speaks Chinese."

I did my best with the limited vocabulary available to me at that moment. Blood seemed to be rushing away from my brain and into my clenched fists. "You are big, and you beat a small dog. You have a bad heart."

At this he laughed even harder. "Foreigner . . . foreigner!" he sputtered through his smirk. I felt enraged enough to do something that would get me expelled from the Peace Corps. I stood, set my feet wider apart, and got ready to throw a punch. I imagined smashing the smile off his face, grabbing the sack of dogs, and leaping off the bus like some sort of SPCA Batman. The man with the shih tzu in hand stood as well and glowered at me. He was about six inches shorter than I was and much skinnier. Still, he looked like someone who didn't really mind getting punched in the face and might even have frequent opportunities to receive these punches. I do mind getting punched in the face. I mind quite a bit.

Advantage, shih tzu owner.

I unclenched my fist. I took a deep breath. I spat at the dog abuser's feet.

His laughter stopped and he shot out of his seat. The glowering of his companion intensified. Remarkably, everyone else on the bus stayed as still as ever. They were watching us as if we were on TV.

"Stupid fucking foreigner," said the man with the sack of puppies, shaking his hand close to my nose. "You're a bastard, and all foreigners are bastards." His face was reddening, and he looked ready to attack.

At this point, the doorman stepped between us. "Calm

down," he told the dog abuser. "The foreigner doesn't understand what he's doing."

"I do understand," I said over his shoulder.

The driver swerved to the side of the road. "Get off," he told
me. "It's for your own good. Take your money back and catch
the next bus." The doorman handed me my two yuan, a look of
genuine concern in his face. I was breathing heavily, sweating
despite the cool weather, and my face felt hot. We screeched to a
stop. I looked around the bus at the other passengers. They were
staring back at me without smiles or frowns, without anger or
amusement. They may as well have been on Valium.

I hopped to the curb as soon as the doorman pulled open
the door. The bus tore down the highway.

◇

I walked the rest of the way into town. It took me about forty
minutes and helped calm me down. I didn't feel good about
how I had reacted on the bus, but I didn't feel all that bad.
Mostly I felt helpless. Part of me wished I had attacked the man.
Part of me wished my Chinese was better so I could understand
what the fuck was going on. Part of me wondered if there was
some irony in heading off to eat fried chicken and getting upset
at a man mistreating his dogs.

I tried to see things from the dog abusers' perspective, but I
had reached the limits of my empathy. I did, however, wonder if
I would ever have the guts to try dog meat. Was I being a prude?
I had already eaten turtle, millipede, and maggot. I had slurped
up brains and bone marrow. Maybe Jennifer was right and I
could even make dog meat seem kosher.

The thought of plunging this far into Chinese culture made
me a bit anxious. Where was the true me in all of this? Rather
than dwell on the question—one that would have required me
to continue thinking about dog abusers and other depressing
aspects of life in China—I tried to think happy thoughts. What

good would it do to obsess on my struggles? This had simply been an indigestible moment. I sighed and tried to put it all out of my mind. The streets were quiet. The city was at the tail end of *xiuxi*. It was a lovely spring evening. I wandered past Internet bars, tire stores, noodle shops, and pagodas. I eventually arrived at the Beijing Hualian and the adjacent KFC.

I pushed open the doors, inhaled the scent of fried chicken, unzipped the jacket I was wearing, and prepared to get into "line." Or, to be more accurate, I prepared to engage in the rugby-style scrum jostling in front of the counter. Guiyang had no orderly queues and no culture of waiting one's turn. Whether at a bank, a bus stop, a hospital, or a KFC, the laws of the jungle ruled. First come was not first served. Instead, it was a Darwinian survival of the angriest.

Most foreigners dreaded getting in line in China. Not me: I relished each little battle. My height and the shock value I created as a Chinese-speaking white person gave me a distinct advantage over my more experienced opponents. I was finding that I could get myself to the front of any line if I was as ruthless as those around me. I had grown to love the scrum.

In fact, I even began to see the Chinese queues as more honest and democratic than those back home in the U.S. In China, you could push your way to the front. In America, you could buy your way forward. I always hated waiting in lines at airports and watching the first-class passengers saunter right past me. As someone with more muscle than money, I preferred the Chinese method of queue jumping.

There were eight people jostling for position in the KFC, attempting to place orders all at once. I took a breath and engaged the mosh pit. I steadily moved my way forward, edging in front of one person after another until I was able to plant my left foot at the base of the counter. With this pivot established, I faked right, and busted out a move I had down so well I could have had it patented: the left-arm-swim, right-hip-thrust. This got me past a businessman yelling into his cell phone and a fat little kid staring at me with saucer eyes. An old lady tried to counter my maneuver by lowering her shoulder into my crotch, but I was too quick for her and smashed her downward with a simple drop of my book-filled backpack. She gave a respectful groan, clearly impressed with my 360-degree awareness, and moved aside. After hip-checking a primary school student, I placed my hands on the counter, elbows angled up and out. I was fully in control.

"*Huan ying guang lin!*" yelled a fresh-faced teenager from behind the counter as she placed a tray in front of me. *Welcome to our restaurant!*

"I want two chicken breasts, a small order of French fries, and a Sprite without ice," I said in Chinese. The teenager began speaking again and looked up, seeing me for the first time. Her voice got caught in her throat. Her eyes widened. She had the surprised look of a soccer groupie seeing David Beckham in person. David Beckham with his hair on fire. David Beckham with his hair on fire and speaking in tongues. I smiled and repeated my order.

The girl behind the counter was speechless, but the old woman I had previously crushed was ready to leap into action. She pushed her head under my armpit so that she could address the teenager: "He cannot understand!" she yelled.

The teenager furled her brow and nodded. "He cannot speak Chinese." She was coming back to life.

"I can speak Chinese," I said in Chinese. "I'm speaking it right now. I want two chicken breasts, a small order of French fries, and a Sprite without ice." I was trying to stay calm and collected. I knew that the old woman and the teenager behind the counter were accustomed to foreigners who could not speak a word of Chinese. I didn't want to take out my anger at the dog abuser on these two women, but I felt my stress levels inching upwards.

The old lady swiveled her head underneath my armpit so she

could look up at me. She laughed a smoker's laugh and yelled again. "He cannot understand!" I briefly considered locking her neck in a vicious Macho Man Randy Savage sleeper-hold—one quick twitch and I could pop that head right off. But I restrained myself and looked directly into her eyes. "I understand," I told her in slow, clear Chinese. "I am now speaking Chinese." Her face, only a few inches from mine, was a mask of excitement. She smelled like ginseng and baby powder.

"No, you're not speaking Chinese," she said, before yelling, once again, "He can't understand!"

I switched my gaze from grandma to the teenager and prepared to try another tactic. Before I could begin, however, I was rescued by the primary school student I had previously hip-checked. She had wormed her way next to me and told the girl behind the counter my order. "He says he wants chicken, French fries, and a Sprite." She looked up at me, red in the cheeks. In English, she said, "Go sit down, and I will bring it to you." I shrugged my shoulders, sighed in relief at her kindness, paid my bill, and swam away from the counter.

A few minutes later, the little girl came to my table, tray in hand. She was even redder than before, trying to work up the courage to speak to me. She looked a bit older than Big and Little Twin. She wore a blue tracksuit, the standard school uniform for Chinese middle schoolers.

I waited for a few seconds, but my volunteer waitress couldn't find the nerve to say anything to me. The Sprite and French fries wobbled precariously on top of the tray. I bailed her out: "Thank you," I said in Chinese. I switched to English for the first time that day to ask her age. With this prompt, her nervousness dissipated, and she put the tray in front of me. "I am thirteen years old." My time in the Wang village was helping; I was getting much better at recognizing the ages of Chinese children. "My name is Sally," she continued. "It's nice to meet you."

Sally and I had a pleasant conversation. She was thrilled to be able to practice her English, and she took the chance to ask me the usual questions: Which country are you from? How long have you been in our China? Do you like our Chinese food? Can you eat our hot, spicy food? Can you use our chopsticks? Do you believe in the God?

In the end, I asked her why she seemed to be the only person who could understand my Chinese. "You're very bad at speaking Chinese," she said bluntly, "and they are not expecting you to use it."

"I feel like my Chinese is pretty good," I told her in Chinese. She shook her head.

"But you can understand me," I said, again in Chinese.

"No, I cannot understand you," she replied in English.

I forced a smile and ate my fries.

❖

Later that afternoon I was ready to head home. I knew that at 4:00 p.m., the trip from the center of Guiyang back to Huaxi would be a bit of a nightmare. In most cases, I would have read in a park, had a cup of bubble tea, or killed time by playing mah-jong with my Peace Corps buddies Nick and Dylan, and our Chinese friend Lulu, and returned to campus later in the evening. On that particular night, however, I had promised some of my students I would meet them for a game of basketball before dinner. I had to suffer through a rush-hour bus trip.

First I tried the 109 but it was not allowing people to board at the stop near the KFC—the buses just kept zooming by, waving people off. I walked ten minutes to the stop for the 203 but it never arrived. Perhaps the drivers were rerouting? There were some benefits to allowing drivers to avoid traffic jams and adjust their routes on the fly, but these benefits accrued to the people already on the bus. Those waiting at the bus stops were out of luck.

After waiting half an hour, I switched strategies again and headed for the 90, another ten-minute walk away. There were about thirty people at the stop when I arrived, and a 90 was just pulling up. The bus looked full, though not excessively stuffed with bodies. I would make my basketball game, after all.

The doors to the bus opened and the thirty people started mashing their way on board as three people attempted to mash their way off. Both the bus driver and the doorman were screaming at the top of their lungs. They were shouting in the same heavily accented local dialect used by my gentle (but not particularly helpful) handyman, Mr. Ma. Our attempts at fixing my shower had once gone awry due to miscommunication, but as I listened to the driver and doorman I suddenly realized I could (mostly) comprehend the Guizhou accent. I understood much of the slang the men were using and now recognized the shifts in tone and word order that had once made life in Guiyang incomprehensible. Mandarin was helpful in Guiyang, but not nearly as helpful as *Guizhouhua*. I would no longer make mistakes like the one I had made the first time I ate hotpot: in an attempt to order meatballs, I asked the waitress to show me her breasts.

Eventually, the scrum worked itself out and the doorman stabilized the situation. He was planning on letting only three people onto the bus to replace the three who had gotten off. This was out of the ordinary. Buses crammed to bursting were de rigueur. That day, however, the doorman had to deny entry. "There's a traffic cop on the highway," he told the frantic crowd, "and I could get a ticket if I carry too many people. Only three can get on board." The others would have to wait for the next bus, though it was unclear when (or if) it would arrive.

I decided not to wait.

I rammed forward with some of the same moves I had used at KFC, boarded the bus, and went to sit down. Some of the people I stepped over looked at me with respect. Others looked at me like they wanted to destroy me and whatever country I came from. I was glad I wasn't wearing my Peace Corps T-shirt.

I sat down. A moment later, the doorman tapped me on the shoulder. "There are no seats," he told me. He had switched from the local dialect to standard Mandarin.

I felt a bit ashamed at my aggressiveness (*Is this how people in first class feel?* I thought to myself) but I wasn't going to move. "I'm going to take this seat right here. I'm sorry for being rude, but I've got to get back immediately."

The doorman nodded, satisfied with my answer. As he turned away from me to collect fares from other customers, the driver leaned back from the steering wheel and yelled to the passengers, "He doesn't understand Chinese!"

"I do understand," I told him with a sigh. "I am speaking Chinese right now. Can you understand me?"

"Of course I can," the driver laughed. "But I didn't think foreigners could learn it. It's very difficult for you."

"Yes, it is very difficult," I grumbled.

He smiled and gave me a thumbs-up. "You speak Chinese very well! You're as good as Da Shan!"

"Thanks," I said as I handed him two yuan. "I'm just happy to finally be on a bus."

The doorman and driver both returned to their jobs. The driver started honking and pulling away from the curb, and the doorman collected money from the other new passengers.

Across from me, a girl leaned over to her father. "He cannot speak Chinese," she whispered. "He is French."

I closed my eyes, took a deep, dust-filled breath, and tried to go to my happy place. It took a while, but eventually I found it. When I got there, people were petting their dogs, fast food was everywhere, all was quiet, and everyone understood me perfectly.

Drafted

The bus ride back to Gui Da got me on campus in time for my basketball date with my students. I had been playing ball every day that month at the courts near my office. The games continued to be laid-back. In fact, they were *too* laid-back; I was itching for real effort and I had been asking around about where to find some stiffer competition. My inquiries had gone nowhere.

That night, however, Kevin pointed me in the right direction. He and I had played dozens of games together by that point, and we often guarded each other. He was one of the better players in his class; he could sink an open-jump shot, he was stronger than most, and he was one of the taller students at the school. At 130 pounds, however, he still felt it appropriate to call me Shaq.

That evening after our games he pointed away from the courts and off into the wooded area not far away. "You have wanted better players," he told me. "That's where you can find them." I followed the direction of his finger. He was indicating Ivan Drago, the stone-faced and strong-jawed giant who had been watching me play basketball since I first set foot on the court the previous September. As usual he was wearing a tracksuit and visor, crouching low, and holding a cigarette between his thumb and index finger. He was watching me coolly.

"Talk to him," Kevin said. "He's been waiting for you."

I swallowed hard and made my way towards Ivan. He remained in his crouch, puffing away. I squatted down next to him and waited for him to speak.

"You're a good player," he said eventually, without moving and without looking my way. He shook a pack of cigarettes my way. "Smoke," he commanded.

"No thanks," I told him. He nodded and tucked the pack into his pocket.

"You are smart," he responded. "Smoking would hurt your game." He pointed with his cigarette at the court. "What do you think of these players?"

"They're not very good," I replied. I had learned to enjoy the blunt assessments that were expected from Chinese teachers. "Still, I enjoy playing with them."

Ivan nodded. "If you are hungry," he said, "I will take you to dinner. I have heard from some people that you like Muslim food, and I am a Muslim. We can go together to a famous Lanzhou pulled-noodle restaurant."

This, I knew, was not a simple offer of dinner. If I accepted, I would be, in some sense, obligated to return a favor. Ivan was developing *guanxi* with me. I decided to reciprocate. "OK," I told him. "Let's go eat."

Ivan took me to a black Ford Focus. The engine was running and a driver was behind the wheel. He wore white gloves. Ivan gave me the front seat and twisted himself into the tiny space in back. The driver rolled out of the front gate of the campus and turned south, away from Guiyang and towards the countryside.

As we drove, Ivan told me more about himself. He was exactly my age—we realized we shared the same birthday. Like Dean Wang, he was originally from Shanghai. The university had brought him in to coach their basketball team. "I'm here studying

Confucianism, but my real task here is as a coach, particularly a basketball coach," he told me. There were a handful of students at the school who were not on the academic track, and he was in charge of many of them. He told me to call him Coach Qin. I got the feeling I was being very politely recruited.

Coach Qin explained that his arrival at the school was part of an effort to up the profile of Gui Da. "The leaders want us to become what we call a 'key university,'" he told me, "but this is very difficult. One way we think we can attain this distinction is through better physical education." He went on to tell me that in Mao's day, schools focused equally on intellectual, ideological, and physical education. Gui Da was going back to the "four-four-four" system: "four hours on becoming an expert, four hours becoming Red, and four hours becoming stronger each day."

Basketball wasn't the only sports push. A new soccer stadium and indoor training facility were in the works as well. Construction at the western edge of campus had already begun. "Within the year we expect that inspectors from Beijing will come to make sure we have made significant progress," Coach Qin told me. School leaders wanted everything in perfect order before the inspectors arrived. If Gui Da earned the designation of a "key university," it would receive huge yearly subsidies directly from the central government. This was part of a national push the Communist Party was undertaking to put its educational spending in line with world averages. In 2005, the average country spent about 5 percent of its GDP on education. China devoted only half that amount.

"So you see," said Coach Qin in a bit of a non sequitur, "it is important for us to have a strong basketball program."

Our driver soon pulled our car off the pockmarked main road and onto a side street. We were out beyond Huaxi, far from Guiyang. The surrounding countryside was quiet and dark. We came to a walled compound and rode through a gate. "This is

Qingyan Ancient Village," the driver told me. "It is a very special place, very authentic."

This turned out to be a bit of an exaggeration. Qingyan was about as authentic as Main Street at Disney World. Most of the original village—including a five-hundred-year-old Buddhist temple, a sprawling garden complex, and a massive tomb—was destroyed during the Cultural Revolution. What I found in its place was a carefully rebuilt tourist attraction. I later learned that the provincial government forced a few hundred Bouyei peasants to move to another city so it could raze their homes and rebuild an approximation of the original Qingyan. The reconstruction had stone streets, wooden storefronts, ethnic-minority art shows, and a plethora of restaurants (specializing in stinky tofu, rose wine, and pig feet). Hundreds of Chinese tourists were bused to the gate of the village each day, where they gathered under a massive poster of Chairman Hu's "Eight Honors and Eight Dishonors." They had to pay forty yuan to enter the town (about six bucks), though Coach Qin had the *guanxi* to avoid the fee. The gatekeeper simply waved us in.

We left the car and wandered the narrow streets. Although Qingyan was not authentic, it was certainly quaint. I felt like I was in an old kung fu movie. Small shops were lit by lantern. Flower boxes lined the sides of the streets. There were dozens of teahouses marked simply with the familiar 茶, the character for tea, and snack stalls with fried potato and watermelon slices. There were terraced gardens with groups of retirees playing mahjong, each wearing thin, blue Mao jackets to ward off an evening chill.

After a few minutes, we entered an unpaved, dirt alley. I peeked into a window and saw the living quarters of one of the store owners. There was a TV blaring a Monkey King movie, a clothesline full of dripping underwear, and a small bed. It was all jammed behind the cash register in this typical business/

abode. Three or four people probably lived in this space, which had the total area of a queen-sized bed.

Coach Qin stopped abruptly. We had apparently arrived. A sign swung in the breeze and had the following written in flowing calligraphy: "Li Mei's Advice House."

"Before we eat dinner, we should have our fortunes told," Coach Qin told me without turning around. He entered the doorway of the Advice House. I followed behind, slightly nervous and totally curious. I had never had my fortune told. I tried to envision what I would find on the other side. I imagined the strange Asian grocery store from the 1980s movie *Gremlins*. Would I find a cute little mogwai for sale that would turn into a demon if I fed it after midnight? Or would I find the dojo where Daniel-san became the Karate Kid? I knew I was mixing my Asian film metaphors.

It didn't much matter which Pat Morita film I conjured because the room we entered was far less interesting than I had hoped. Lit by a few bare lightbulbs, the room was mostly empty except for a small table in the corner with stools on either side. The table had an old tapestry thrown over it with an image of a dragon. "Go sit," Coach told me. "I'll find Li Mei. She's the best fortune-teller in Guiyang." He disappeared out a back door without another word.

I stood blinking for a moment, waiting for my eyes to adjust to the gloom. The floor was well-swept wood. The walls were exposed brick. There was a shrine towards the back of room and broken yellow incense sticks littered the floor beneath it. The air smelled sweetly of soil.

Eventually, I moved into the corner and tried to sit on the stool. It was not meant for an American. It stood about four inches off the ground and was at most five inches wide. Perhaps— perhaps—a Chinese midget could sit on this stool comfortably. As I lowered myself onto it, however, my left knee seized up and

I heard my L5 vertebra pop, no doubt a residual consequence of being thrown around on the basketball court an hour earlier. I toppled backwards, frozen in a half-sitting, half-standing repose. Coach Qin and Li Mei entered the room to find me sprawled on the floor clutching my back. I jumped up quickly, dusted myself off, and took a look at my fortune-teller.

The first thing I noticed was Li Mei's height. Standing at her full stature—limited by a twisted spine that caused a severe hunch—she barely reached my belly button. She was also balding. She wore a dark blue bandana, an embroidered smock, and rope sandals. She had exactly three teeth and her face was weathered to a leathery dark brown. In other words, she looked like someone a Hollywood casting director would choose for a Chinese fortune-teller.

Meanwhile, Li Mei assessed me with what seemed like mild disgust. Her nose crinkled and her brow furled. Did I stink? She began to speak and Coach Qin translated rapidly, surprising me with his adept English.

"He has good *su zhi*," she said in a dialect I couldn't recognize. "That much is clear without any help." Li Mei lurched towards the shrine and grabbed a rolled leather parchment tied with a thin string. I looked at Coach and asked him what *su zhi* meant. He told me it means something like "class" but he couldn't think of a more direct translation.

Li Mei unfurled the parchment on the table. With a black background and white lines connecting triangles, circles, and hexagrams, it looked like the interdimensional map from the Terry Gilliam movie *Time Bandits*. She motioned for us to sit. Coach sat on the stool that had almost killed me and I sat cross-legged on the floor. I marveled at the ease with which Coach folded himself onto the tiny stool. His legs, torso, and feet joined together in a trick of human origami. A lifetime of squat toilets made the Chinese as flexible as gymnasts.

"Your fortune is based mostly on your animal year," Li Mei

began as she shuffled to the back of her shop to pour some tea. "You, I can see, are a dragon." I hadn't told her that. Perhaps I looked my age. Or perhaps Li Mei had magical powers. At that moment I would have believed it. She handed me a cup filled with tea leaves and pulled a steaming pot out from underneath the table. She poured me a drink and ran her hands over the parchment. A crooked finger stopped on top of one of the hexagrams.

"This is the *khen*. Your *khen* represents what is original, adventurous, and firm. This is where your fortune begins."

I sipped my tea as Li Mei turned to Coach Qin. He was looking back at her in rapt attention. They chatted quickly for a few minutes. The tea was pungent and hot and warmed me against the damp chill of the small room. After a few minutes, Coach told me he had instructed Li Mei to learn about my health and the fortune I would bring to the people around me. He had also told Li Mei my birthday and my job. The fortune-telling could now begin. Li Mei took a deep breath and began speaking slowly, referring occasionally to a small book that I later learned from Coach was the *Yi Jing*, or, as it is often written in English, the I Ching. The book was a source of Taoist wisdom, astrology, cosmology, and geomancy. In the hands of an expert, it could reveal the future. Li Mei told me my fate:

"Most dragons, according to the *Yi Jing*, are powerful men. This diagram can help me see what you—that dragon—should do and what you should avoid. Because of your birthday, we begin your journey in the third nine, undivided." She pointed to one of the hexagrams on the map in front of her. I had no idea what she meant, and Coach didn't seem to want me to ask. He was translating rapidly, focused totally on Li Mei.

"From this place, a dragon must remain active and vigilant during the day, and in the evening become trusting and open. There will be occasions after dark for you to be humble and to try new things. If you are not careful, your arrogance will harm you in the nighttime."

Li Mei paused and sipped from her own cup of tea. Coach took the moment to look at me and smile. I noticed how soft his face became when he smiled, a stark contrast to the sharp angles of his usual stony visage.

"The dragon has always been an emblem with the Chinese of the highest dignity and wisdom," Li Mei continued. "It is an independent creature. The dragon emblem runs through all of your many hexagrams so you may be *too* independent. If you do what you are meant to do, you will have great luck and bring fortune to those around you. But in *your* future, it is clear you will exceed the proper limits. The line should not be always pulled tight; the bow should not be always kept drawn. You must know when to retreat. Beware of overinvolvement." Here, Li Mei leaned forward and made eye contact with me for the first time. She repeated herself: "Beware of overinvolvement."

The fortune-teller leaned back and smiled broadly, giving me a terrifying glimpse of her three teeth. The monologue was over.

"Thanks," I said in Chinese. "But I don't understand."

She laughed and told Coach she could make things much clearer. "Join the basketball team," she said. "There you will find adventure and glory. Other options will result in a loss of money."

Li Mei clapped her hands together. "You should trust me," she said, rubbing her palms against each other. "And I don't even want to get paid. This advice is free."

Coach was nodding. He looked relieved. He had brought me to Qingyan as a recruiting trip; he brought me to Li Mei to con-firm his instincts. Coach and Li Mei began chatting again. I took out my notepad and wrote as much of the monologue as I could remember. While I didn't believe in the power of the *Yi Jing*, I saw why Li Mei had such a good reputation in Guiyang. She was confident, almost mesmerizing. Before leaving her shop, I prom-ised her I would remember her advice.

Coach and I went with our driver to the Muslim restaurant

he had promised. It specialized in dishes from Lanzhou, the capital city of Gansu Province far to the north. We ordered *da pan ji*, which literally means "big plate of chicken." The family that owned the restaurant quickly got to work, mother chopping vegetables, son kneading and pulling dough into thick noodles, and father pressure-cooking a whole bird. As we waited for the meal, we ate sunflower seeds and drank warm beers. Coach was friendly and relaxed, and we chatted in English. By the time we popped the bottles on our second round, I felt like I was sitting with an old friend.

The *da pan ji* arrived at our table about an hour after we ordered it. The chicken was dripping off the bone. Potatoes, red and green peppers, onions, and carrots mingled with the chicken bits in a fragrant, brown sauce. Star anise, garlic, and fennel sat at the bottom of the steaming pan. We dug in, eating in silence for a few minutes. I was absolutely famished. When we had made a dent in the mound of food, our waiter brought us the noodles he had hand pulled. He dropped them into our pan, giving us another pile of food to devour. I waited for the noodles to soak up some of the sauce, then began slurping them up. Coach was leaning back, sipping his beer, and patting his belly. Our driver was enjoying a post-dinner cigarette. We were all glowing.

"Good food?" Coach asked simply.

"Perfect," I said, taking one last bite of chicken.

"Are you full?"

"Stuffed."

He leaned forward. He had waited all evening to pop his question. Here it came: "You know that I am the basketball coach. I know that you enjoy playing." Coach grabbed the last piece of chicken with his chopsticks, popped it into his mouth, and smacked his lips. "I hope you can be drafted to join our team."

I nodded. "My pleasure."

Coach smiled and raised his glass. "*Ganbei*," he said, drinking the last of his beer. I wasn't sure how a teacher could play on the college team, but this was precisely what Coach Qin had arranged. I was a varsity athlete for the first time since high school.

十五

A Lesson
from Australia

My basketball career began in Coach Qin's apartment. A month
after our trip to the ancient village, he invited me and my new
teammates over to his apartment so we could meet each other
and collect our uniforms. He had cooked up more Lanzhou
noodles, this version served in a soup broth with thin strips of
lamb. I sat with my new teammates, slurping at the noodles and
drinking Pubu, a brand of beer that is to Guiyang what Yuengling
is to Philly: a cheap, watery, locally brewed way to kick back
with friends. The green, liter-sized bottles of Pubu had pictures
of Huanguoshu Waterfall, Guizhou's greatest tourist attraction.
I had heard various superlatives about the falls. Jackie told me it
was the largest waterfall in Asia. Dean Wang told me that "more
water flows from Huanguoshu than from any other source in
China." Shitty told me, "Every year, many people die jumping
into the water." None of these statements inspired me to visit.
Huanguoshu sounded too much like Guizhou's version of Wall
Drug in South Dakota, or the St. Louis Arch. You go, you look,
you take a picture and maybe buy a snow globe. Then you go
home.

The waterfall did not interest me, but the beer that bore its

name had the team feeling good. I assumed that the other players would be surprised to have a foreigner joining them, but this
was not at all the case. In fact, I wasn't even the only foreigner in
the apartment. Greg, a forty-something Australian with yel-
lowing teeth, thinning hair, and hunched shoulders, was in the
corner of the living room working hard to get himself drunk.
Four empty Pubus sat before him, and he was halfway into his
fifth. Coach must have seen the half-surprised, half-concerned
look on my face because he quickly pulled me aside and explained
Greg's presence: each team in the city was allowed to have one
(and only one) foreigner, and while many teams didn't have
access to this allowance for diversity, Gui Da had always had one
white boy. For the previous two seasons, Greg had been studying
Chinese at Gui Da and playing on the team. I had taken his slot,
making this something like his farewell dinner.

Greg was drinking alone, but everyone else was chatting,
sharing food, and clinking their bottles together in toasts to
health, hoops, and money. The team was happy to have me on
board, and I was glad to be in a room full of men. I had gotten
used to my classroom, an estrogen-rich environment that was
90 percent female. Most of the girls I taught fit snugly into the
Hello Kitty Asian stereotype. Cute was the ultimate goal in
everything from fashion to body language. My students wore
T-shirts with cartoon sheep on them, adorned their book bags
with pieces of flair, and emitted exaggerated sighs at the mention
of boy-band pop stars. The most famous of the stars, a singer-
actor from Seoul named Rain, was a smooth, doe-eyed nymph
with flowing hair and a silky voice. He had the title role in a
drama called *Sang Doo, Let's Go to School!* Imagine *Saved by the
Bell*, if every episode was as Special as the Very Special Episode
in which Jessie admitted she was addicted to caffeine pills. Every
hour of *Sang Doo* seemed to end with Rain standing by the ocean
in a tuxedo, bow tie undone and shirt unbuttoned to reveal his
perfectly smooth chest. He would stare longingly into the eyes

of a rail-thin, weeping, cartoonish costar. All of the girls in my class had seen *Sang Doo, Let's Go to School!* in its entirety, and had learned from it the importance of crying softly when boys were unkind.

A room full of beer-drinking athletes was a big change. I had forgotten how nice it could be to hang out with the guys. We played quarters. We told bawdy jokes. We arm wrestled. Gui Da was a world away from Cornell, but a case of tall boys blurred the cultural differences between college life in China and America.

Greg eventually stumbled over in my direction and flopped down on the couch next to me. We had met a few times before in the strange ways foreigners in Guiyang all came into contact with each other. Whenever I passed him on the street or saw him on a bus I was overcome with the awkwardness of having either to greet this relative stranger simply because he, too, was white, or walk by him with fake nonchalance. Either way, I felt like a phony, and I usually decided to say hello. The stilted conversations that followed went something like this: "Hey," I might say.

"Hey," Greg would respond. "Nice day today."

"Yup." Pause. *Long* pause. And handshake. "Good talk, Greg."

Part of the awkwardness of Greg's presence came from my feeling that he was invading *my* city. I wanted to be the special one-and-only representation of the foreign. It was very un-PC (un–Peace Corps, that is) but I couldn't suppress the enjoyment that came with being something of a celebrity in town. Greg was a total buzz kill.

Still, I apologized to him for taking his spot on the team. "I didn't realize there was a quota on foreigners," I explained. "Coach just let me know that since I'm in, you're out."

"Forget it, mate" he told me. He really called me *mate*. I nearly laughed. I wished I could pour him a Foster's and hand him a koala bear. "I'm heading home soon anyway," he continued. "I've already fucked enough Asians to last a lifetime."

I stared at him in silence. "Pardon?" I finally managed.

"Oh, don't tell me you're one of these missionary prudes," he said, swigging his beer and groaning. "Good-looking guy like you should be knee-deep in pussy out here." Our teammates were busily engaged in their own conversations. Coach Qin was probably the only one who could have understood us anyway. Still, I felt my neck reddening in embarrassment.

"Nope, not a missionary. Peace Corps."

The Aussie scoffed. "Ah. A do-gooder. Look, kid, you've got to realize you can't help these people. They'll take what they need from you even if you don't want to give it, and they'll reject anything you think they need." A long sip of his beer bottle. "Believe me. I've been here for years and nothing has changed."

"Little bitter?" I asked quietly.

This elicited a sneer. "Why should I be? Like I say, I've gotten laid more than I ever did back home."

"Greg," I said, "That's really . . . awful."

Greg slowly turned his head towards me and looked me up and down. He had genuine pity in his eyes. I felt simultaneously disgusting, disgusted, and confused. How could someone this pudgy, shuffling, and rough around the edges throw pity at me? He looked like a B-version of Tom Waits after his worst hangover.

"Mate," he repeated, "You can't help these people. The culture is thousands of years old and totally disinterested in changing." He finished his bottle of beer and grunted at someone to bring him another. "The Chinese know how to get what they want out of foreigners. They want you to be rich and white and share the wealth. That's it."

Coach Qin, playing the good host, delivered Greg a beer. There was no bottle opener handy, so the Australian bit it open and finished his thought: "I give my students what they want." Greg smiled at me and stood to use the bathroom. I was left to wonder both how he had bitten open a beer bottle and if it was possible to come to China without an agenda. Greg came for sex. Others came to bring Jesus. Others came to make a buck. What had I come for? What was my agenda? I had thought surprisingly little about these crucial questions. I pondered Greg's blunt statements as I sipped my beer, thinking of Rain's final words in *Sang Doo, Let's Go to School!*: "We never know how our actions will change people. We can only live with an open heart." Rain was onto something, but without an ocean to stand next to and a full body-waxing, I would never be much like him.

◇

After we finished our noodles and beer, Coach distributed the team gear. I was given two jerseys—red for home games, yellow for away games—and a team wristband. My jersey had the same number as the old Celtics center Robert Parish: 00.

I took my shirt off to try on the jerseys. My teammates howled when they saw my chest hair, and some came over to pet me. It was in this way that I met the other four starters on the team: Ah Ge, our team captain and point guard; Shui, the tallest member of the team; Da Bao, a chubby and powerful forward whose nickname meant "Big Dumpling"; and Chen Chen, a smooth talker with well-coifed hair and fake Ray-Ban sunglasses.

Ah Ge ran his fingers through my chest hair, smiled broadly, and said, in stilted English, "Nice to meet you!" He had a wiry, muscular body and twinkling eyes. He would prove to have boundless energy on the court and a killer crossover dribble. He looked a bit like the smiling figure in all of Yue Minjun's paintings. I immediately liked him. The other starters also ran their fingers through my chest hair and greeted me. Before long I would know their games inside and out: where Shui liked to receive the ball in the post; Da Bao's rapid-fire pump fakes; Chen Chen's showman's skills in practice and total unreliability in games.

For now, it was just four strange men rubbing my nipples.

After receiving our uniforms, we all exchanged cell phone numbers. There would be no schedule of games or practices. Instead, in typical Guiyang style, Coach would simply call us a few minutes before something important was going to begin. If we could make it, great. If not, no hard feelings.

A week or so later, I received a text message telling me where to go for our first practice. I was in the middle of lunch and had already eaten a heaping bowl of fried rice. My distended belly made me feel singularly unathletic as I raced home to grab my sneakers. I laced them up and headed out of my apartment towards the courts.

Practice with the Gui Da team turned out to be similar to every other basketball practice I had ever attended. We ran, we practiced our shooting, we walked through some plays. The only major difference came in our strength training. It took place in a drafty, crumbling building next to a dilapidated, grassless soccer field. The building was half full of fifty-gallon burn barrels and what looked like old munitions. Cracked windows let in just enough light for me to see that a small part of the floor space was given over to a prison-yard-quality weight room. Rusty barbells sat next to rickety weight benches and cobweb-covered stretching mats.

Ah Ge led us through our exercises. Most of them involved picking up something heavy and moving it up and down as quickly as possible until either exhaustion or injury occurred. When I showed the team some of the ways I was used to lifting weights, they shook their heads in disappointment. My slow, controlled, and careful movements were totally unimpressive. "This isn't tai chi," Chen Chen told me. "It's weight lifting. You should behave more like *Shi Wa Xin Ge*." He was referring to Arnold Schwarzenegger, whose Chinese name roughly translates to *Ten Times the Man You'll Ever Be*. Chen Chen proceeded to bend over and grab a weight that was far beyond his strength. He heaved, back muscles bulging, and managed to twist it over his head. I could practically hear his tendons snapping, and I was once again stunned by the difference between my perceptions of safety and those of my Chinese friends.

Each day for nearly three weeks we lifted rusty barbells and ran up decaying stairs. I made sure only to eat light meals in case of a sudden text message with instructions. I managed to show up to most of what Coach Qin planned, and learned a few of the team's basic plays. We also met a few times for beers. Ah Ge taught me how to trash talk. I learned to say *fangpi ba ni*. Literally, "You farted."

By early June, we were deemed ready for competition. We would play in Guiyang's Key League against other colleges, a few company teams, and a couple of military bases. It was the best competition the province had to offer, the equivalent of America's Division I. I was nervous: pickup games at Gui Da were one thing; the Key League would be another story.

十六

The Taiwan
Problem

Our first game was scheduled for a Saturday night against the Guizhou Military Academy. We donned our yellow jerseys and boarded the team bus at 3:30 p.m. It was the first hot day of the early summer so we had all of the windows lowered. Dust and gravel mixed with the cigarette smoke of my teammates. I tried not to breathe too deeply.

An hour later, we arrived at our opponents' gym. It was by far the nicest court I had seen in China. The floor was made of wood (rather than the usual concrete), the rims had nets, and the baskets seemed actually to be regulation height. The gym had seating for a few hundred spectators, and the stands were about half full. On the wall near the entrance was a life-sized photo of Yao Ming dunking on a player from the Japanese national team.

I scanned the crowd. I had invited Jennifer and Vivian and spotted them at midcourt. They waved to me in unison. To my surprise, I also saw Big Twin, whom I had seen several times on subsequent unannounced visits to her village. As my team-mates sat on the bench, I called her over. She scurried down the bleachers and approached the bench, red in the face.

"I'm so happy to see you!" I told her. She was wearing a Houston Rockets T-shirt and had her hair in pigtails. She looked adorable. "How did you know to come to the game?"

"I'm a big NBA fan," she told me. "And everyone knows you are now on the team. I'm excited to see you play." Word travelled fast in Guiyang. I gave her a high five, told her I'd stop by the village soon, and returned to my teammates.

We began warming up by running laps, stretching, and shooting free throws. Eventually, Coach Qin called us over. He had been a fairly ruthless taskmaster during practice and had an even more serious look on his face today. He was giving complex commands and speaking rapidly. My Chinese had gaps in basketball terminology but the physical language of the sport was not lost in translation. I was never more than a half step behind his instructions. Or so I thought. Ultimately, I was just nodding and hoping that once on the court I could figure out how to be a part of our offensive and defensive schemes. This strategy had worked when I played basketball while living in Israel. My teammates spoke Hebrew, Arabic, and even Russian, but we never had trouble working as a unit. I hoped the same would hold true in China.

"Take a look at the other team," Coach told us. "We will not be covering number 11." Coach Qin looked at me to be sure I understood, and he spelled it out clearly for me: "He is high up in the Communist Youth Party, so he must be allowed to score."

"I got it," I said. "Be friendly with number 11." Coach nodded at this and gave me a thumbs-up.

Number 11 would have clear paths to the hoop as a consequence of playing basketball in a place where *guanxi* ruled. Relationships took precedence over winning. I had already been told to expect a sliding scale from the officials. Older players would be given more leeway than younger players, and party members the most leeway of all. Everyone else, however, could be attacked at full intensity.

Coach went on to explain our strategy for the game (aside from allowing Communists to score) and then announced the starting lineup. I prepared to take the court.

As I stepped towards the center circle for tip-off, the previously noisy gym fell silent. The early-summer air seemed to thicken. Fingers pointed at me and brows furled. I began feeling acutely self-conscious, which was nothing new in China, though in this case there was something sinister about the way the officials and the players on the other team were staring at me. The crowd seemed happily curious, but my opponents seemed downright hostile.

The two referees quickly held a private conference. After a few moments, they called over the coaches. After a few more moments they called over the captains from both teams. Ah Ge ran off to join the meeting. What was amiss?

Finally, after more than ten minutes, my coach broke from the growing huddle and walked in my direction. He put his hand on my shoulder.

"You cannot play here," Coach Qin said, looking mildly embarrassed. "You must leave."

"Why?" I asked.

His response, delivered after a pause and with a long breath, "The Taiwan Problem."

I was taken aback. "I don't understand," I said with genuine confusion. I was, of course, well aware of the Chinese belief that Taiwan, a fully independent island-nation off China's east coast, was a renegade secessionist province. I was also aware that this was a sensitive diplomatic issue, and was one of the "Three Ts" Peace Corps volunteers were warned to steer clear of in conversation (along with Tibet and the Tiananmen Square Massacre). Still, I didn't have a clue why Taiwan was coming up as we were preparing to tip-off.

Coach explained: "You are American, and the American military supports Taiwan. So you are not allowed to play here in

this gym at the military college." As he spoke, his mild embarrassment was turning to full-blown shame. He seemed to realize how petty this seemed.

"Oh," I said, trying to maintain a smile. "You know, I'm not
in the military. I'm in something called the PEACE Corps." I
emphasized the word "peace." Coach just shook his head.

"Well, can I at least talk to the officials?" I had long ago learned
that in Guizhou, a city far from Beijing, far from "Opening and
Reform," a city with *guanxi* flowing through the streets and with
chauffeurs doubling as fix-it men, a city with pork-filled Shabbat
dinners and with students named for human anatomy; in such a
city, no rules really existed. There was always a way to find a compromise. Everything was negotiable.

The "rule" banning Americans, I was quite certain, had been
created moments ago during the meeting of the officials and
coaches. But for me to dodge the "rule" I would need to figure
out what was motivating its sudden creation. Were the Chinese
worried about an American beating them? Was my coach being
punished for some political mistake he had made? Had the U.S.
just announced a sale of weapons to Taiwan? Or was the referee
simply a dick?

My coach motioned for the refs, and one of them—a Chinese version of Ichabod Crane—slowly swaggered over, jaw set
rigidly in place. He had the proud look of a man with very little
power and a sudden opportunity to wield it. He held his head
high, trying, and failing, to make himself taller than me. He
was able to convey quite a lot with his body language: China is
powerful, said his face. You must respect us, said his puffed
chest. Don't Mess With Guizhou, said his beady eyes.

"Hi!" I smiled broadly, while patting him on the shoulder. My
Chinese skills limited my ability to bargain, but I was determined
to do my best. "I know the Taiwan issue is sensitive," I told him,
"but basketball can build friendships. Please allow me to play."

Ichabod was unresponsive, so I added a sentence I expected

would be a bombshell: "An Australian played at this school last year, and Australia also supports Taiwan. Why could he play while I cannot?" I hated to drag Greg into the discussion, but it seemed like a reasonable question. He had played a game in this very gym not six months ago without any difficulty.

Ichabod seemed to look at me for the first time. "That was different," he said. His eyes had a combination of amusement and scorn. "We thought he was from Xinjiang." Xinjiang is China's massive and sparsely populated province in the far northwest, colonized by Han Chinese in recent decades to the growing resentment of the indigenous Uighur Muslims. Why would Ichabod claim Greg was Uighur? It seemed like a ridiculous stretch, but as my coach later explained to me, "Americans and Australians have blond hair and blue eyes, but Greg has black hair, so he looks Uighur." I have neither blond hair nor blue eyes, and I pointed this out to my coach. "No," he told me as he looked at my brown hair and green eyes. "You do have blond hair and blue eyes."

Back to my negotiation with Ichabod: I decided to alter my tactic to fit his ethnic creativity. "Well, I'm not really American," I said, preparing to play my trump card. "I'm Jewish. Like Karl Marx."

This ruffled Ichabod. He looked me over carefully. Could it be true? Was this a real Jew in front of him? He didn't seem to know what markers to look for. Perhaps he was nervous that my clever Jewish ways would lead him into a trap. Perhaps he was worried that he could not ban any brethren of Comrade Marx from the gym. He started stuttering and his head shook on the end of his long, thin neck. My coach was looking more and more miserable with each sputtered word.

I decided to be merciful and bail out Coach Qin. Any improper action on my part would reflect poorly on him, and I didn't want to get him in trouble.

"Well, never mind," I said with a wave. "I love China, and I will just watch the game."

The ref quickly regained his composure, turned on his heels, and went back to the circle of Chinese men that had moments earlier enacted my ban. They chatted quietly. Ichabod soon returned, barely concealing a smile. "You must leave the gym immediately. A car will be provided to escort you from the grounds of the military school." He spun again, and Coach Qin gently coaxed me off the court. He kept his hand around my shoulder and began quietly rambling an apology as he walked me towards the door. "I am sorry for this, but you must understand. The Taiwan problem ... military ... unification ... so sorry."

When we reached the door, he sighed and shrugged his shoulders. "You'll be able to play next week. We won't be at the military school." I walked out into the now-cool evening air. As the doors to the gym swung shut, a uniformed police officer standing in the evening twilight lit a cigarette, blew the smoke at me, and pointed to a car. "I guess you're my driver?" I asked him. His only response was to enter the car and start the engine.

"Take me to the Gui Da," I said. The driver grunted and we tore off in a cloud of dust.

I hummed the Chinese national anthem as we drove. He didn't join me.

A few weeks later, I returned to the Wang village. I wanted to see what Big Twin had to say about my banishment from the gym, and to invite her to our upcoming game which would be held at a neutral site at a gym near the Guiyang train station. I walked slowly. Summer vacation had begun the week before and most students had cleared out. Campus was quiet. I was looking forward to a few months with a happy new rhythm of basketball, Chinese study, and relaxation. It would be nice to have some free time.

As I approached the village, I saw Wang Number One, the twins, and cousin Wang throwing rocks into the river. They ran to greet me, yelling "Hello!" in English. Three of the girls were wearing the white and red uniforms from their school, Minority Middle School #2. Big Twin, however, was in beige nylon pants and a grey T-shirt. I wondered if she, too, was on summer vacation, though I didn't understand why her sisters wouldn't be, as well.

"Why aren't you wearing your school clothing?" I asked Big Twin when the girls reached me.

"Because," she told me breathlessly, "I was too busy with

that." She pointed up the hill to the spot where the girls had been playing before I arrived. A picnic basket sat under the tree in which I had once found myself trapped. "I made dinner for everyone so we could eat on top of the mountain. Now you can join us!"

"Lucky me!" I replied. "What are we eating?"

"Nothing too special," Big Twin told me, "though we have some traditional Bouyei food. Maybe you're not used to it." She took hold of my hand. "We should all hurry up the mountain now before it gets too dark." We were lucky to have the long days of early summer. It would remain light until around 9:00 p.m. I nodded and we were off.

Wang Number One led the way, bounding up the hill. Next was Little Twin, followed by Big Twin and then me. Cousin Wang stayed right at our heels. We followed a well-worn path on the northern edge of the village. It went through a small garden, past a now-barren field, and into the gingko trees at the base of the mountain. The girls knew the path and walked quickly. It took a lot of concentration for me to keep up with them without tripping over the roots and rocks on the steep incline.

Big Twin spent much of the walk peppering me with questions. When is your next basketball game? Do you know Allen Iverson? What is your favorite NBA team? Can you dunk? Do all Americans love basketball? Most Americans are fat, but you are skinny; is this because you play basketball? Can we come to Gui Da and play with you? Is Yao Ming better than Shaq? I answered her questions in rapid-fire succession. Big Twin wasn't kidding when she said she loved basketball. I told her I would send a text message to the family's cell phone when I found out the date, place, and time of our next game. She cheered when she heard this. "I hope you are very successful," she told me. "Go, Mike, Go!"

Big Twin also spent some of our hike teaching me the Chinese nicknames for her favorite NBA players: Dirk Nowitski was *Deguo Zhanche*, the German Racecar. Carmelo Anthony was *Tian Gua*, or Sweet Melon. Tim Duncan was *Shi Fo*, the Stone Buddha. My favorite nickname, however, had to be that of Dikembe Mutombo, the seven-foot-three Congolese center. He was known as *Feizhou Dashan*: Big African Mountain.

"Iverson is my favorite player," Big Twin told me, "because he is so small but plays with such a big heart. I also like his haircut and his tattoos. He's also very handsome."

The other girls groaned. "He's much too black," Cousin Wang yelled from behind us. Wang Number One agreed. "You can't trust African people," she told us. "They are dangerous."

Big Twin ignored the other girls. She wanted to meet Allen Iverson. "Since you are from Philadelphia," she said to me hopefully, "maybe you know Iverson?" I was so out of breath from our climb I could only shake my head.

Big Twin eventually bored the other girls with her questions about basketball and they told her to quiet down. They had questions of their own and curiosity about other aspects of life in the United States. They were particularly curious about life for American minority groups and seemed to have been given the standard "Jimmy Is a Black Boy" education. They truly believed race relations in the U.S. hadn't much changed since Reconstruction.

While the Wang girls' ideas about minorities in the U.S. were outdated, they were still far ahead of what I had known about ethnic diversity in China before arriving in Guiyang. I always assumed China was simply full of Chinese. Among my students, however, were Bouyei, Miao, Hui, and Uighur, ethnic groups that were distinct from the majority Han. China officially recognized the existence of fifty-six ethnic groups and five religions within its borders (Protestant Christianity, Islam, Buddhism, Taoism, and Catholicism). It was all part of what could be called Identity Politics with Chinese Characteristics.

The Wang girls introduced me to the intricacies of the subject. "Han Chinese don't really like us Bouyei," Wang Number One told me at one point. She got a nasty stare from Cousin Wang, who quickly disagreed, saying, "China takes care of its minorities."

Cousin Wang explained: "In school, we learn that our Communist Party is building a lot of things for the Bouyei people, and is helping us become more modern and scientific."

"Is it true?" I asked. She shrugged. I followed up with another question: "What do your parents say about this?"

Cousin Wang shook her head. "I never asked them. I don't think they can understand, because they never went to school."

"America hates its minorities," Wang Number One interjected.

"I don't hate minorities," I replied.

She slapped back my experience with a phrase I had heard before: "We have learned it." Yvette Chen once used this phrase when telling me about Michael Phelps, the swimming Jew; Shamus used it when telling the Guj about the American hatred of old people. Wang Number One, like Yvette and Shamus, had learned something from a teacher or a textbook, and, in a country where both of these sources were generally trusted without question, the lessons had become bedrock assumptions. It was nothing a quick conversation with me could dislodge.

Along with questions about race relations, the girls also wanted to know about music, film, and fashion. Cousin Wang took one look at my iPod and squealed with delight. She popped in the earbuds and started flipping through my music, pausing when she hit Justin Timberlake, the Black Eyed Peas, and Michael Jackson. She sang along to "Beat It," dancing her way up the path. An iPod would likely cost more than her family earned in a month.

"Are there any Chinese stars who are famous in America?" she asked, speaking too loudly over the din of the earbuds.

"No music stars," I replied.

"Not even Li Yuchun!" she cried, looking up at me. I shook my head. The girls were horrified.

"But we know about Yao Ming," I told them, hoping to save China some face.

Little Twin snorted. "He's not even very popular in China anymore. Now, we all love Liu Xiang." Liu, a handsome, single, patriotic twenty-four-year-old was, indeed, the hottest athlete around, having won a gold medal in hurdling in the 2004 Olympics. He single-handedly transformed China's perception that Asians are racially incapable of sprinting as fast as Africans. His upcoming events in the 2008 Olympics in Beijing were being awaited with an anticipation that fell somewhere between the way I felt in the days before *The Matrix: Reloaded* was released in theaters and the way *Left Behind* readers feel when they think about the Rapture. I felt pity for the runner: anything short of gold and he would be a national disgrace. The old racial theories would, no doubt, return.

"Who is the most beautiful Chinese woman?" Wang Number One asked me with a blush.

"I think Zhou Xun is very beautiful," I told her, thinking of the lead actress in my favorite Chinese film, *Beijing Bicycle*. The girls hadn't heard of her. They hadn't heard of Gao Yuanyuan, Zhao Tao, or any of the other women I had seen in the Chinese movies I had bought on pirated DVDs. They were more familiar with American stars than the homegrown variety: J-Lo, Britney Spears, Julia Roberts, and Madonna were their favorites. The only two Chinese stars we all knew were Gong Li and Zhang Ziyi, both of whom the girls hated. "They look like prostitutes," Big Twin told me.

The hike revealed that while Wang Number One was the leader of the group, each of the girls had quite a bit to say. Cousin Wang asked, "What people are you?" I told her I was an American, but this answer was, apparently, inappropriate. "Lo lo lo!"

she said in English, missing the mark on her "n" sound, before switching back to Chinese: "I know *that*. What *people* are you?"

I took a guess at what she was looking for, assuming she was returning to her favorite topic: ethnicity. "I'm Jewish," I said, beating them to the next line, adding, "just like Comrade Marx." All the girls nodded their heads with approval.

The conversations with the Wang girls that afternoon were the easiest I had ever had in Chinese. It was the first time I actually forgot I was speaking a foreign language and just let the words flow. This had more to do with the girls than it did with me. They were far less guarded than my students or colleagues at Gui Da. They were unendingly patient with my questions and with what must have struck them as some strange gaps in knowledge. They were also less befuddled by my broken syntax and grammar than my older friends. The word order in Chinese was still difficult for me. I imagined I sounded like a Chinese Yoda ("old Madonna is, but dance she can"). It didn't seem to be a problem for the Wang girls. They listened intently and made sense of what I was saying. If my mistakes were egregious they would offer gentle corrections, but for the most part they could decipher even the most brutally hatcheted sentences.

We continued up a barely visible path. It was steep, thin, and overgrown with vines. After about twenty minutes we stopped for a break. Little Twin quickly scaled a tree and, from twenty feet above, began raining golf ball–sized purple fruit down on us. The other girls ran around catching the fruit. They showed me how to peel them and eat them. "Do you have winter peaches in your America?" Big Twin asked me. I shook my head. This small, succulent purple fruit was new to me. Little Twin remained in the tree, eating from a perch in the branches. After I had a few bites of peach, I climbed up after her. "Be careful," Big Twin told me with a laugh. "Don't get stuck again."

I found Little Twin poking a caterpillar with a stick. "I am a better tree climber than you," I said with a wink. She smiled and narrowed her eyes. She pointed to a taller tree next to the one we were in, and indicated a challenge. I nodded, and we descended together.

The girls tittered as they surrounded the other tree, waiting for our contest to begin. "Be careful!" they yelled at me. Then, without warning, they yelled, "Go, go, go!" I grabbed Little Twin and tossed her away from the tree, intending to begin my climb with a few seconds of advantage. She cried out with surprise and laughter, but her sisters lunged at me and hugged my legs to prevent me from taking the lead. I tickled them until they collapsed, losing precious moments: Little Twin was halfway up the tree by the time I began. I started climbing but was no match for my opponent. While I carefully checked for hand- and toeholds, Little Twin rocketed upwards. By the time I reached the top of the tree, huffing and covered in sap, she was smiling sweetly at me, hiding something behind her back. "What is it?" I asked. She revealed a soggy, rotten peach, which she lobbed at my head. Since my hands were gripping the tree for dear life, I could do nothing but let the peach smack me in the forehead and ooze down the length of my face. This was the prize for finishing second.

◇

Eventually, we reached the top of the mountain and sat for lunch. We had a fantastic view of the valley below. The air was clean, and the sounds of China were far behind us. There were no honking cars, no students yelling Crazy English, no Chinese opera ... nothing. Just the gentle waving of ginkgo and pine trees. I had forgotten that quiet is a feeling as much as a sound. The mountain path seemed like a tomb at first, but as my ears adjusted I heard the bugs and the breeze.

The girls had prepared fried eggs, potatoes, and *kugua*, a bitter melon popular in Guiyang, particularly among the Bouyei. We also ate pork jerky and steamed buns. We ate slowly, chatting the evening away. Wang Number One eventually lit a small fire to keep us warm. She used old newspaper and pieces of plastic for fuel.

◇

We made our way down the mountain after dark, entering the village by moonlight. I paused at the rear gate of the village to wave good-bye, but the Wangs would have none of it. "You should come to our house for tea," said Wang Number One. I happily accepted the invitation. Our group walked single file down the narrow streets. The center of the village was a maze of high courtyard walls. I had no idea where we were going. Before long, however, we reached the Wang house. Their front yard was cement and gravel. Two dogs were chained to a pigsty at the far end. Four massive pigs were snoring away. The only other things in the yard were a clothesline and a long bench pushed up against the wall of the house. Next to the bench was a door, and at the door was an impossibly old-looking woman wearing the traditional blue hat and smock of the Bouyei, an outfit similar to the one the fortune-teller Li Mei had worn. The woman in the courtyard had wrinkled skin, gnarled hands, and cloudy eyes. She mumbled something I did not understand and disappeared inside. The girls rushed ahead and bounded into the house.

When I got to the doorway, I scanned the dim interior. I saw whitewashed walls and a tiled floor illuminated by a single bare lightbulb. There was a TV at one end of the room, tuned into a movie channel, and a dilapidated leather couch at the other. There was also a small refrigerator with a few old books on top. In the middle of the room was a coal-burning stove that doubled as a table. During the winter, the family would no doubt spend a lot of time huddled around the stove. Beyond the main room was the kitchen. I heard the old woman shuffling around inside.

Wang Number One soon emerged from the kitchen with a boiling kettle. She served me a deliciously bitter tea and offered me some sunflower seeds. The old woman emerged from the kitchen as well and watched me from the doorway. "That's our mom's mom," said Little Twin. She and Big Twin were on the couch next to me munching on sunflower seeds, spitting the seeds on the floor. I asked the girls if they would ever wear a headdress like their grandmother's. They all shook their heads. "Too old-fashioned," said Big Twin. "Our teachers at school tell us we are not allowed to look like that," added Little Twin. "We need to adopt scientific ways to develop the New Socialist Country-side."

I tossed a few sunflower seeds into my mouth. "New Social-ist Countryside?" I said as I chewed. "What does that mean?"

Little Twin shrugged. "I don't know. It's just what we believe."

We paused and sipped some tea. "Where are your mom and dad?" I asked eventually.

"Working in Chengdu," Wang Number One told me. "They will be home in a few months for Grave Sweeping Day." Momma and Poppa Wang were typical workers among the other billion, travelling hundreds of miles to find seasonal work in factories and at construction sites. It was either this or the backbreaking work of traditional farming. I knew the girls would someday face the same choice: tend to a small farm in the Guiyang mountains and live a subsistence lifestyle or enter the global-ized industrial workforce. The only hope they had to escape this unsavory choice was through education. I hoped they were studying hard.

I spit some shells on the floor and sipped my tea. We sat together in silence watching the movie on the TV. It was Schwar-zenegger's *The Terminator*.

十八

Nabokov, Pynchon, DeLillo

Most of my teaching hours at Gui Da during my first year had been spent introducing basic English skills to Kevin and his class of college sophomores. Progress was slow, but the work was fun. I had certainly noticed President Bill's critique of China's students: my undergrads focused a lot of energy on preparing for state-administered standardized tests and had to be convinced that creativity, debate, and analysis had educational value. Nevertheless, when given the chance, Kevin and company were flexible and willing participants in the activities I designed. By the end of our first year together, his class was diving into any opportunity I gave them to be playful. They translated Chinese fairy tales into English and performed them. They organized a poetry slam. They sang and danced without prompting. The stereotype of the robotic Asian math whiz—a stereotype President Bill reinforced—was wrong. These teenagers were every bit as goofy and fun-loving as those I had taught back home.

Dean Wang called me into his office a few weeks before the new term got started. "Your students have a lot of fun," he told me, in what struck me as far less than full-throated praise. He followed up with a proposition: the dean wanted me to start teaching an additional class, this one at the graduate level.

"We've never had an American teach the postgraduate students," he told me. "But I have told the department you are capable." The topic of the class was right up my alley: postmodern American literature. I was flattered by the offer and agreed to take on the extra teaching. Dean Wang sent me on my way, promising he would let me know more of what he had in mind as soon as possible.

I waited for more information on the new class as my undergraduates returned to campus. Most had gone home to their villages for what they called "self-study," though a few had found summer internships in Guiyang. Yvette, for example, worked at Pizza Hut. "I work ten hours a day," she told me, "and my feet always hurt. Still, I am grateful since jobs are difficult to find and in this one I can sometimes use my English." To my horror, Yvette told me she had been paid only one yuan an hour, or about fifteen cents. She rebuffed my shock with a slightly mangled— though apt—cliché: "Don't look a dead horse in the mouth," she told me seriously.

It was good to have everyone back on campus again. Little seemed to have changed for Kevin and his peers. There was, however, one glaring exception: Kitten came back to campus with bone-white, albino-quality skin. She had been bleached over the summer in an expensive and painful cosmetic process. It terrified me to look at her unnatural glaze, but I was in the minority. "It is so beautiful," Shitty told me.

"Why do you think so?" I asked her.

"We have learned it."

"Learned it where?" I asked. Shitty looked at me like I was asking her where she had learned to speak Chinese. White was beautiful, and that was the end of the discussion.

◇

As classes settled into a routine again, the gingko trees began to lose their leaves and the fields surrounding the university fell into an autumn hush. One morning—the last day of the season with weather warm enough for me to open my office windows and let in some fresh air—I had a new visitor. He quietly pulled open the door as I sat listening to chickadees chirping in the courtyard just outside the Foreign Language Building. There weren't many birds in Guizhou. In 1959, Chairman Mao had designated sparrows as one of the "Four Pests" along with cockroaches, mosquitoes, and rats. The sparrows, he believed, were eating the seeds his farmers were planting and thereby harming national grain yields. The cockroaches, mosquitoes, and rats were equally pestilent and all needed to die.

Cockroaches, mosquitoes, and rats survived the purge. China's sparrows, however, were wiped out after peasants spent months in the fields killing them and banging pots and pans together to disrupt their mating. By 1960, Guizhou was not only sparrow free, but entirely bird free. As a result, grubs and other crop-killing pests went about their business predator free. They decimated local crops. Mao ultimately had to beg North Korean dictator Kim Il Sung to give him a few sparrows so he could repopulate China's fields. Ah, Chairman Mao! How wacky!

The man who visited my office that morning sat quietly and listened with me to the chirping birds. The students who were sitting in my office when he entered immediately jumped up and offered him their seats. He was apparently something of a big deal and they treated him with extreme deference. He was short, thin, and had a desperate comb-over. His bald head was shiny and mottled. He looked to be about fifty years old. He had a curt, direct manner, and carried himself lightly on his feet. "I am here to interview you," he announced. My students scurried out of the office.

"An interview?" I was my usual two steps behind. "For what?"

"To teach the graduate students," he replied. "My name is Professor Fei, and I am the head of graduate studies here."

"Nice to meet you," I told him, extending my hand, which he gripped tightly. "I'm surprised we have not met before."

Professor Fei held on to my hand and sized me up. "Yes, I have been gone. I was on sabbatical at Sichuan University last year," he said with obvious pride. Professor Fei smelled of tobacco and had ink stains on his fingers. He struck me as the equivalent of an American professor in a corduroy jacket with elbow patches.

Fei, I would soon learn, was a big shot on campus, one of the only fish bigger than Dean Wang. This was largely because he had his PhD from Beijing University, China's top school. His presence at Gui Da would be a little like a Yale professor moving on to teach at DeVry Technical Institute.

Professor Fei ran the graduate studies in foreign languages at Gui Da, and he ran it as a private fiefdom. The program was more or less shut down for the term of his absence and students were told to put their studies on hold until he returned. Now that he was back, he wanted to get a firsthand look at the new foreign teacher. Was I just another missionary, using Gui Da as a front for my true interests? He peppered me with abstract questions, starting with the Bible and moving on to probe my understanding of technical terms (structuralism, postmodernism, deconstructionism, etc.) and names (Nabokov, Pynchon, Heller). I kowtowed appropriately.

"Why do you think Americans love the Bible?" he asked, near the beginning of the interview. He followed up with an insightful question: "Does one need to understand or read the Bible to understand Western culture?" I answered both questions vaguely, saying something about treating holy texts as literature. He seemed to like the answer. He also liked the fact that I was Jewish. "Many great scholars are from the Jews," he told me, "and many great bankers, as well." I nodded.

Eventually, Professor Fei told me I would teach "ten lectures on masterpieces of postmodern American literature." I would teach two masterpieces per month for the fall term.

"Well, that's really great," I said. "But I'm not sure what you're looking for, exactly."

"You will teach the masterpieces," he repeated.

"I'll do my best," I said. "But to be honest, I need more guidance." I asked him which "masterpieces" he had in mind.

"You should teach the masterpieces of Nabokov, Eliot, Hemingway, DeLillo, Pynchon, and Heller."

I raised my eyebrows. This was as expressive as I allowed myself to get in meetings with high-level officials. "Can the students read all of this in such a short time?" I asked.

"You can tell them the content of the material and how to interpret it," he replied. "They do not need to read it themselves. To be frank, that's not very important."

I was stunned. I would be teaching students pursuing graduate degrees in American literature and they were not expected to read the literature itself. Was this Teaching and Learning with Chinese Characteristics? I wasn't sure, but I took the job despite my discomfort with Professor Fei's expectations.

◇

I was once again thrown into the classic Peace Corps dilemma. Where was the line between imposing a set of values in the manner of the White Man with a Burden, and introducing a new, potentially better way of thinking? I wanted my students to read and interpret; I didn't want mere regurgitation. At the same time, I wanted to embrace my role as a humble Peace Corps volunteer. I was meant to listen, to integrate, and to scrupulously avoid the assumption that I knew best.

I needed some advice. I asked Jennifer if she thought I should follow Professor Fei's instructions or my own instincts. "I know it's important for the students to know what 'experts' have to say," I explained to her, "but I think it's equally important for them to have opinions of their own."

Jennifer found my ideas a bit muddy. "Why do they need to read the books for themselves?" she asked.

"Well, for one thing, it is what our class discussions will be based upon."

"But what is there for them to discuss? They don't know anything. You are the expert, so you should just tell them what to think."

"That's basically what Professor Fei said." I sighed. "But it seems like a lousy way to learn."

Jennifer adopted a measured tone for her response. "Your methods are interesting, but it's not the Chinese way. We believe before you are qualified to offer your opinion, you should know what all of the experts believe. You should copy them again and again until you know their thinking. Only then can you build on it."

I was sitting with Jennifer at a new bubble-tea shop near campus. It had opened over the summer, replacing a hot-pot restaurant. The Chinese characters identified the shop, quite simply, as the *Taiwanese Style Bubble Tea House.* For some reason, however, the English name written in gigantic blue letters on the store's exterior read "Fashion Bar Sexy." I stirred my bubble tea. Jennifer's explanation of the Chinese teaching method made a lot of sense. Too much sense, in fact; I sat down with her, confident I could explain the importance of teaching critical reasoning and independent thinking. But I was suddenly off balance. Was it arrogant to think I could have important ideas? Was it naïve to believe my students would learn more from speaking to each other than they would from memorizing the words of the experts?

I ate a tapioca ball and had a momentary educational identity crisis. My undergraduate students had a lot of fun during our first year together and we got to know each other quite well.

Many of the students made strides with both their pronunciation and oral comprehension. All of them had gained confidence. It was safe to say, however, that my lessons on topics such
as "slang as heard on *Friends*," and "the importance of the glot-
tal stop" hadn't gotten them to do much deep thinking. Was I
content to be nothing more than a volunteer speech coach?

I thought of Yvette's first visit to my office and her paper
"Great Jew," and of Jackie's difficulty controlling the volume of
his voice. I thought of the oft-repeated phrase, "We have learned
it." I thought of the computer-science major who believed
America hated old people. I thought of Jimmy the Black Boy. I
also thought of President Bill's assessment of China's schools.
What in the world had I done for a year? I was suddenly struck
by the evidence of my overall ineffectiveness.

"I understand what you're saying, Jennifer," I finally told her,
"but I just can't teach that way, at least not to PhD candidates." I
would try for more.

She shrugged. "Give your way a try," she told me. "But don't
expect too much. Even postgraduate students aren't used to
this. They may criticize you for it."

We sat together for a few more minutes before I paid the bill.
I headed out of Fashion Bar Sexy and dropped by an Internet
café. With a few hours of work, I had assembled a decent dossier
for the students. It contained excerpts from a few key novels
(*The Sun Also Rises, Catch-22, Lolita, One Flew Over the Cuckoo's
Nest, Cat's Cradle*), as well as poems, a few short stories, song
lyrics, and reproductions of postmodern art. The postgraduates
might not be able to find copies of all the literature we would
read, but at least they could get a sense of the language.

To get the reading packet ready for the students, I had to ven-
ture to the fourth floor of the Foreign Language Building and
into the cluttered office of Ms. Zhou, the keeper of the printers
and copiers. The old Xerox machine was only a few generations
beyond carbon paper. Ms. Zhou guarded it the way Frodo

guarded the One Ring. She looked me as I entered the room, narrowing her eyes.

"I hate to bother you," I said, stumbling over my words, "but I've put this packet together, and I need copies for the students in the postmodern literature class." Ms. Zhou was sipping tea out of a brown porcelain cup with a lid. She removed the lid and steam surrounded her face. She took a slow sip and replaced the lid with an aggressive clink. She placed the cup on top of a teetering pile of papers and snatched the packet out of my hand. She looked it over.

"What is this?" she asked dismissively.

"Just some American fiction. Professor Fei has asked me to give some lectures . . ."

"Fhu," she breathed. "I know. But which fiction will you teach?"

I was surprised at the question, but I told Ms. Zhou my reading list. She looked up at the mention of *Lolita* and, in English, quoted the opening of the book: "Lolita, light of my life, fire of my loins. My sin, my soul." I stood in stunned silence.

"I studied literature," Ms. Zhou explained. "It was more trouble than it was worth." She shooed me out of her office, promising me she would deliver the packets to my students as soon as they were ready. I backed out of her office without a word.

◇

As promised, my students arrived for their first class with their packets in hand. They sat quietly, papers neatly organized on the tables in front of them, pens at the ready. None had an eye patch or, according to the roster I had been given, a strange English name. All looked at me expectantly. I suddenly froze.

My teaching confidence was low at that particular moment because of a meeting I had with Kevin earlier in the day. He had come to my office hours to show me the textbook he was using for his class, Introduction to Western Culture. The text was called

A Survey of Britain and America. It taught him that "the U.S.A. is a highly developed country with modern science, yet it is also a country of religion, in which people have religious fervency." Kevin had underlined the sentence and asked me for my opinion.

"It's a bit of a generalization," I told him.

"But it is true," he responded.

"Um . . ." I stumbled. "Well, it's true that the United States has a lot of religious people."

Kevin nodded and narrowed his eyes. I felt like I was stepping into a trap. I quickly skimmed the rest of the chapter to see what else Kevin had learned and how my response might result in unintended consequences.

Fervency, Kevin had read, came in many forms in America. The Quakers, for example, "might have been one of the great American sects, but they are too peaceful. . . . They take no interest in politics, but they are greatly respected." He also read that Jews suffered from "strong built-in prejudices of the Protestant majority" that hindered their participation in public life. According to the text, neither Jews nor other minority groups could ever hope to become president.

The section on religion ended by explaining that "religion has much influence over the people. Modern American religious freedom in the law is often counterbalanced by a spontaneous social pressure in flavor of religion."

Kevin had taken dutiful notes in the margins and underlined key words. He had written questions. One of the best, etched in his flawless handwriting, was "What is religious flavor?"

To this I had no answer. "I think this is a lousy textbook," I told Kevin, after helping him with some vocabulary words and explaining that "flavor" was probably a typo: "favor" made a lot more sense. "The book is far too one-sided."

"That might be," Kevin admitted, "but it still has information I must know for the upcoming tests." Kevin showed me a short essay he had written summarizing the text. He was asked to name the causes of social problems in America. "There are several causes for them," he wrote.

> Firstly, films, TV programs, and novels are full of robbery. . . .
> Second, the laws in some states are not severe. . . .
> Thirdly, there is a constant corruption of the police. . . .
> Fourthly, guns are privately owned. . . .
> However, the most important reason is the capitalist system in America. In the capitalists society, although science and technology is highly advanced, some people are suffering from spiritual hollowness. They start to look for things curious and exciting. Therefore, only when the American capitalist system is ended, can all these social problems be solved.

"Do you believe this?" I asked Kevin.

"I must learn it," he responded.

"But you don't have to believe it."

He thought about this for a moment. "I don't have to believe anything," he told me. "But I know what I have to learn. So that's what I must do."

This just about summed up the limits of my teaching. There was a point beyond which I had not yet pushed. As I stood in front of the postgraduates, confronting my chance to finally do more, I worried I would not be up to the challenge. A long minute ticked by in silence.

Finally, I stammered out an introduction and began. Class went slowly that first day. The students were tentative. Few spoke up. My lesson plan was built around ferreting out the differences between the modern and the postmodern. It was no easy task, and it fell flat. We covered some of the basics, but I ran out of gas and ammunition with about twenty minutes left in the two-hour period. I told the students to use the rest of the time to do some in-class writing. They handed me their notebooks as they walked silently past me and headed off to dinner.

◇

I took the pile of papers to my favorite restaurant on campus and sat down at my usual corner table. I ordered a bowl of lamb, potato, and peppers over thick slices of noodle, a dish I knew would cheer me up a bit. To make the dish, the restaurant owner's son took a log-sized chunk of dough in one hand, a curved knife in the other, and shaved bits of the dough directly into the boiling broth that he used to cook everyone's food. The broth was in a twenty-gallon pot at the entrance to the restaurant and was heated by a honeycomb-shaped brick of charcoal. After shaving in my noodles, he placed a top on the pot and began preparing the meat and vegetables. Within a few minutes, he fished the noodles out of the broth with a long-handled colander, dumped them in a bowl, and piled the meat and veggies on top.

I had a fresh, hot, delicious plate in front of me with a free side of broth to wash it all down. I couldn't order a beer at the restaurant—like most pulled-noodle joints, this one was owned and run by strict Muslims who eschewed alcohol—but the owner had assured me I could BYO. I bought two cold bottles of Pubu at the shop next door, asked the owner to open them for me, and took out the pile of essays. I figured the beer was all that could help me get through the short stack of papers. After a few minutes, however, I was so engrossed that I set the beer aside. I read from the first essay to the last in rapid succession, sitting in rapt attention for more than an hour.

The essays ranged in style, coherence, and focus, but one theme ran throughout: freedom, my students agreed, is available internally or not at all. The students expressed a nuanced sensitivity to the "Lost Generation" that presaged postmodern literature. Hemingway and his contemporaries of the 1920s were, like many young people in twenty-first-century China, living in a world that seemed unmoored from traditional values. Liu Xing, a twenty-eight-year-old man from a village about a twenty-hour bus ride away from Guiyang—deep in the countryside—wrote, "The only values in China today are money and power. I have no desire for these things. I am so lost, just like Ernest and Eliot." By "Ernest," Liu Xing meant Hemingway; Eliot was T.S.

"I have only obeyed my parents," Liu Xing went on. "I do not like this school, but they have insisted that I stay. I really don't know who to follow, but I do not trust myself to be my own guide." Liu Xing was the only male student in the class. He had the loneliest look in his eyes I had ever seen.

One of my other students, a second-year graduate student named Isabel, wrote the following:

> Postmodernism is suicidal. As we know, Hemingway took his own life. This is the result of being a lost generation. I know that life is difficult in China, and that life is changing very fast. But if we hold to our traditional values, we will become stronger. We must love our families and respect our traditions. I will not become lost. I believe that the sun also rises for us. . . .

I was taken aback. This was far beyond my expectations. Isabel had been one of the few students who spoke up during the first class. She had jet-black hair that ran straight to her waist. She was tall, thin, and had worn a well-tailored, beige cotton dress. She was urban, classy, and confident.

The most interesting essay in the bunch was written by a student named Qing Fong. She had not said a word in class. Instead, she had looked at me, unblinking, with piercing eyes. She had not raised her hand or made a sound. It had been unnerving.

Qing Fong wrote in simple, elegant sentences. Her writing referred to a joke from a David Foster Wallace reading we examined in class. The joke was about a fish swimming with a buddy through the ocean. An older fish swam by and said to the two young fish, "Water's nice today." The younger fish keep swimming for a while before one paused, turned to the other, and asked, "What the hell is water?"

"It is difficult for me to write about my own culture," Qing Fong began. "Like the story of the fish, I cannot see the water. But I do know that this water was poisoned long ago. I think most of us are simply trying to survive. Call this survival whatever you wish. I will work to make the water clean again."

I had to figure out a way to get these postgraduates to say in class what they were comfortable putting on paper. I had a new goal and restored hope for my second year of teaching.

十九

Every Dream Can
Become Your Dream

One morning about a month into the term, Jennifer surprised me at home, ringing my doorbell soon after I had eaten my breakfast. "I want to buy an apartment," she told me as soon as I opened the front door, "but I don't know if it is a good idea. Can you give me some advice?"

I stared at Jennifer, dumbfounded. What advice could I offer? Jennifer grabbed my arm and started pulling me out the door. "We're going downtown," she said. "We will have some tea, and discuss my plans." I barely had time to grab my keys and my man-purse. I had picked up this fashion accessory from Chinese businessmen, another puzzle piece in my attempts at integration. We were quickly on our way.

During the forty-minute bus ride from campus into the center of town, Jennifer explained why she thought I might be able to help advise her with this momentous decision. Her parents grew up in a China without banks and without private ownership; none of her friends had ever taken out a loan; Jennifer herself had never bought anything worth more than a few hundred dollars. Yet she lived in a city that told frequent stories of young Communist cadres getting rich quick, a city with two

Walmarts, and a city with a growing entrepreneurial mind-set. "Things are changing fast," Jennifer told me. "Our Communist Party is now encouraging us to buy private property. Perhaps this is a new Chinese Characteristic."

I could see why Jennifer felt ill equipped to navigate the quickly changing economic landscape. She had never learned the history of her country—the textbooks about China were just as absurd as *A Survey of Britain and America*, and just as immune to questioning—nor had she read the political philosophy that supposedly undergirded her national ideology. She was born when Mao was still in power. She was now being encouraged by his heirs to dive into the very waters he tried to helm the Chinese ship right past. Her friends were confused, her parents were overwhelmed, and her teachers were tentative. I was the only person she could turn to for what she described as "advice about capitalism."

So advice I gave. The first thing I told her was the first thing my parents told me when I bought a condo at Eighth and Addison in center-city Philadelphia: "Don't get in over your head." This was not what Jennifer wanted to hear. Real estate was hot in Guiyang, prices were skyrocketing, and anyone who wanted to move up the ranks in the Communist hierarchy was expected to buy property and buy it quickly. Speed was the primary issue; cost was a secondary concern. "A new law has been passed," she told me, "so we are now allowed to own a home. We must get one quickly." All of the upwardly mobile wanted in, and everyone was worried they would be priced out and left behind. Speculators were swooping in.

As the bus rumbled past the Wang village, Jennifer gave me more details about Guizhou's new economics. A decade earlier in so-called "key cities" like Beijing and Shanghai, property laws had been liberalized. For urban elites on the coast there had been years of de facto private home ownership. Interior China was finally being given the green light.

"We are now allowed to own the buildings, just like the people in Shanghai," Jennifer told me, "but still not the land. That will always belong to the party, and to the people, as Chairman Mao intended. But they will give us a long-term lease, ninety-nine years. This is the new Communism, the new stage of Opening and Reform."

The boom of Beijing and Shanghai was knocking on Guiyang's door as shiny (though shoddy) condominium complexes sprouted up all along the river at the center of town. Units were selling long before they were even finished. The big players in town were buying dozens of apartments and leaving most of them empty, speculating on a continuation of the boom. Jennifer didn't want to waste another minute.

We arrived at Think Fine Tea, a Starbucks knockoff not far from Walmart. Like Fashion Bar Sexy, it served Taiwanese-style bubble tea. Jennifer knew I liked the place and offered to buy me a drink. I ordered an iced jasmine tea with tapioca pearls. Jennifer ordered a coffee.

"If it was possible, I would borrow money from my family," she told me as we sat down. "But to be frank, borrowing money is not a Chinese thing to do." To our left, a pair of high school students were flipping through magazines and sending text messages on their phones. To our right, a Guiyang yuppie smoked a cigarette and stared into the distance. I noticed he had a stack of brochures in front of him, each touting the merits of a different apartment complex. He, like Jennifer, was on the hunt. This may have explained the vacant look in his eyes. He was probably considering spending more money on an apartment than his parents had earned in a lifetime, all on the faith that the Communist Party would stick with its movement towards private ownership. If he didn't buy now he would be frozen out (politically, if not economically); if he did buy now and the political or economic winds shifted, he would lose everything. The top brochure on the table had bold Chinese characters reading, "Your Happiest

Days Are Ahead." English lettering emphasized this message: "Every Dream Can Become Your Dream."

Jennifer sighed. "My parents want to help me buy a home, but the prices are just too high for them." She lit a cigarette and blew the smoke towards the ceiling. She had learned not to bother to offer me a chance to smoke, though she still considered my abstinence somewhat scandalous. ("True friends smoke together," she once explained. I told her I didn't want to get cancer. She demurred with the same logic I had heard in Chengdu: "In Guiyang, the air is so toxic that cigarettes are good for you. They make your lungs much tougher.")

Jennifer's parents could not help her, but she could help herself. "My job is good, and I have *guanxi*, so I can get a loan from the bank. But what if the party wants to take the property back? I would lose everything. This is why I need your advice."

I shrugged. "I have no idea what to tell you. I really don't know what's going on in the real estate market in Guiyang."

"Well," she said, stamping out her cigarette. "Let me show you." For the second time that day, she took me by the hand. Jennifer was by far the most forward, aggressive woman I had met in China. For the rest of the day I followed her on a tour of properties she was considering.

It was an eye-opening afternoon. I usually noticed Guiyang's poverty rather than its wealth. The city was nestled in a river basin between barren, unforgiving mountains. The soil beneath the city, as in the rest of the province, was famously lousy; most of the province's peasants were literally dirt poor, eking out a living on a few acres of land. Guizhou Province had no useful natural resources, no trade routes bringing outside money or interest, and very little human capital. All we had was Huanguoshu Waterfall. Nevertheless, my tour with Jennifer revealed a city on the make. Nearly every corner in the central part of town had a showroom for a new high-rise condominium complex. They had names like "European Happiness," "Greenwich Village," and, inexplicably, "The Paris Commune." Each showroom had a 3-D model of the future development, complete with LED lights, fake trees, and tiny little figurines happily wandering about. Thin, porcelain-skinned women in form-fitting traditional silk dresses handed out advertising brochures and color copies of apartment floor plans. Jennifer noticed I was more impressed with the human—rather than architectural—models, all of whom had silken hair, long eyelashes, and shy smiles. She punched my arm at one point, a gesture she had learned from me. "Don't be naughty," she told me, shoving a brochure in front of my eyes.

The pitch in the brochures was always the same: buy now while things are still under construction, because the prices will just keep going up. There were no publicly available estimates on housing prices in Guiyang, but Jennifer insisted that prices on new units had risen about 5 percent a month for the past five years, all in anticipation of the new property laws. "I must buy soon," she said, "because the rising prices will never stop. The government will not allow it." I knew prices couldn't go up forever, but who was I to predict the outer limits of the bubble?

"Who is profiting from all this?" I asked as we exited one of the showrooms.

Jennifer shrugged her shoulders. "I don't know." She was unsure who was building the condos, who was selling them, and who was financing their construction. Jennifer was politically connected but economically naïve. She seemed to be going about her real estate hunt the way I buy property when playing Monopoly.

◇

After wandering all afternoon, Jennifer and I stopped for a snack. The evening light was fading when we arrived at Pen Shui Chi, a traffic circle surrounding a fountain at the center of town.

This was the heart of commercial life in Guiyang. Towering over the fountain was the city's trendiest mall, Modern Capital. The anchors of the mall were the Pizza Hut and a Nike store. Billboards of European models looked down their glossy noses at us. Beneath the models, barefooted children in blackened, Dickensian clothing raced around the traffic circle on homemade skateboards topped with massive wicker baskets. They filled the baskets with recyclables, fighting for empty bottles. I saw a girl who looked a lot like Little Twin reaching into a trash can to pull out a Sprite bottle. It depressed me to see someone so young working as a recycling scavenger. I was glad the real Little Twin would avoid such a fate.

Jennifer and I shared a few sticks of barbequed lamb covered in dried hot peppers. I was tired, but Jennifer, as always, seemed bursting with energy. She was wearing a paisley dress with a thick yellow belt and red high-heeled shoes. Her hair had a slight perm and was frosted with golden highlights. She had carefully plucked her eyebrows. Jennifer fit in well with the impeccably well-groomed Pen Shui Chi crowd. Like most Guiyang yuppies, she got her fashion signals from Western (as well as Korean and Japanese) media. Her outfits, like those of the models in haute couture advertisements in *Vogue*, had nuance beyond my comprehension. For Jennifer, the more bizarre the item, the more un-Chinese and genuinely Western it seemed. She wasn't alone. A stroll in the Pen Shui Chi neighborhood always felt to me like walking in a Michael Jackson fantasy camp, circa 1988: ripped denim, puffy jackets, fluorescent leather, and stiletto boots were the norm. After decades of harshly enforced fashion uniformity—blue Mao jackets for everyone—the explosion of color, textures, fabrics, and layering made sense.

"How much do you spend on clothing each month?" I asked Jennifer as we ate our lamb kebobs.

She sighed. "Too much. Out of the five thousand yuan I

earn, I think I spend almost half!" Five thousand yuan was about six hundred dollars. That was an excellent living in Guiyang, and apparently enough to think about buying a new condo. "I have been buying less clothing recently," she continued, "because I must save for a down payment. I really must buy a home."

There was a long pause in our conversation. I watched the street kids cruise around on their homemade skateboards. Two young boys were wrestling over an empty Sprite bottle. One slapped the other in the face and ripped the bottle free. The second boy barely flinched and went looking for another. The little girl watched the scuffle from a few yards away. She really did look heartbreakingly similar to Little Twin. Eventually, Jennifer broke the silence. "Vivian will go to Beijing next year to live with her husband."

"Her *what*?" I cried. I had known Vivian for more than a year and had heard nothing about a husband.

Jennifer was looking at me with an indecipherable expression on her face. "Vivian is married. Her husband lives in Beijing, so she is very pleased. She will be able to move to that city on his *hukou*. Few Guizhou girls are this lucky." The *hukou* was something like a national ID and it tied Chinese to their place of birth. This kept the cities from becoming Mumbai- or Mexico City–style urban nightmares. Beijing had no shantytowns since Chinese from the provinces were not legally allowed to move to the cities. Vivian, however, could now get to the big city since she could be tied to her husband's *hukou*.

Jennifer lit another cigarette and took a long drag. "She doesn't love him, but he has a good job and this is best for her future. To be honest, I am a little bit jealous. Vivian's marriage is the reason I want to buy an apartment. I don't want to keep renting our current place, because next year it will feel too lonely." She sighed. "Life is always changing. There is no way to understand anything."

We finished our lamb and waited for the bus to arrive to take us back to campus. It was full, as usual, but there were a pair of tiny plastic stools we were able to sit on in the aisle between the seats. Jennifer was finally losing steam. Her shoulders slumped, and she closed her eyes.

"I will be very sad when Vivian leaves," she said quietly. "I will be all alone."

Jennifer leaned against me as the bus rumbled away. The farther we drove, the more she moved from her standard giddiness into something that bordered on morose. As this malaise overtook her, she, like many of my Chinese friends, moved our conversation towards a topic that was taboo with anyone other than a foreigner: religion.

"You are lucky, because as an American Jew you have something to believe in. But what can Chinese believe in? We do not have the God."

"I don't know if I believe in God, either, Jennifer. You know that."

She nodded. When God came up at Guj meetings, I was always honest about my beliefs. I explained that I participated in Jewish culture and did my best to follow Jewish tradition because doing so made me happy, not because I believed in God or the literal truth of the Bible. "I know that you don't believe in the God of most Americans," she told me, "but I think you still believe in more than I do." The bus swerved, and Jennifer was momentarily thrown into my lap. She giggled and returned to her tiny stool. "You have told us that soon you will stop eating because you have a Jewish holy day."

"That's right," I said. "Next week is Yom Kippur."

"This is a wonderful day!" Jennifer was perking up again. "We Chinese need to have something like this. We are losing all of our Chinese days, like Mid-Autumn Festival and Grave-Sweeping Day. We don't even understand Spring Festival any-more. We have forgotten our traditions. But Jews still have them after thousands of years." We were two stops away from campus. The bus slowed to pick up a pair of villagers carrying a bag full of chickens between them. We were directly across the highway from the Wang village. Jennifer was nodding her head.

"I have an idea," she told me. "I will also stop eating for the Jewish day."

I laughed loudly, surprising Jennifer and the passengers around me. I quieted down and lowered my voice. "That's not necessary, Jennifer. Why would you do that?"

She was nodding more vigorously. "Because I can have some meaning on that day. This is what China lacks, and what I lack. I can have meaning. I am too fat, and I have been using the Gui-yang Diet Clinic, but this will be a better way." Jennifer had been heading into town a few times a week to get shots from one of the city's many weight-loss centers. She was an on-again-off-again diet addict. In fact, nearly all of the single women I knew at Gui Da, from teachers to students, and from young to old, used some form of crash dieting, often promoted by snake-oil salesmen from bigger cities. "Look like the women of Shang-hai in only a few months"; "No more ugly"; "Round in the wrong places? We can help!" These were some of the ads I saw plas-tered around town. The dieting, like Kitten's bleaching, was part of the downside of post-Maoist fashion freedom.

"Jennifer, Yom Kippur is not a diet," I explained. "It's a Day of Atonement."

She was unconvinced. The stress of house hunting, com-bined with the impending loss of her roommate, left a Jewish-sized hole in her autumn plans. Yom Kippur was her salve. "I pledge to stop eating," she told me with finality.

She had created another cross-cultural hybrid: a Chinese woman in Guiyang fasting to lose weight as a Yom Kippur pledge. Like Frankenstein's monster, it was a combination of parts that didn't quite fit together. Once animated, however, it could prove uncontrollable. Jennifer's hybrid, I knew, was no more or less odd than a white guy from San Francisco lighting incense in his fancy loft apartment and practicing tai chi. It was globalized spirituality, both beautiful and meaningless.

Everything in
Its Right Place

Monday, Wednesday, and Friday mornings were spent with my undergraduates. We continued to play games and work on pronunciation. Tuesday evenings were reserved for my postgraduates. They were coming out of their shells, though I deserved little of the credit. Once they got used to a conversation-based class it was as if a dam had broken. I simply stood out of the way and let the water rush by. Each class was better than the last. As I learned more about the students I became more comfortable challenging them with both taboo questions and teaching methods they found unorthodox. They responded by debating with me, with each other, and wrestling with their own ideas.

Isabel, I learned, was a Radiohead fan. A year earlier, I had sworn to myself that I would bring Bon Jovi to the people. I had failed, but Isabel's musical taste let me know my expertise might not be necessary.

"I don't think people in Guiyang can like Radiohead," she told me. "But in my hometown, Shanghai, they are more popular. Sometimes when I go home, I feel like I am visiting another country—we have a different dialect, different food, different music, different style. China is more like Europe than the U.S.A.," she concluded. "It is many little countries all together."

"So Radiohead has no hope in Guiyang?" I asked. She shook her head.

"The old people only like Chinese music," she said dismissively. "The young people out here only like pop like Michael Bolton or Céline Dion. I think this music is garbage!" I thought of my Sichuan opera–singing neighbor and his dismissal of kids in Guiyang; he agreed with Isabel's scorn, though from traditional rather than emo-hipster snobbery. Still, I agreed with both of them. Michael Bolton sucked.

A month into the term, she wrote me a short essay analyzing the first track on the Radiohead album *Kid A*. "This is certainly postmodern," she wrote. She was especially interested in the repetitive lyrics to the second verse in which Thom Yorke, the band's lead singer, sucks on a metaphorical lemon before telling the listener that everything is "in its right place."

"With these simple words," Isabel said in class after repeating the lyrics, "the singer lets us know that life is always sour. It has no meaning. And this is all we can expect from it." On that particular day, Isabel was wearing a T-shirt that read, "This is certainly not a T-shirt." I asked her if this was postmodern irony. She looked down at the writing on her chest and smirked. "I hadn't thought about it," she responded. "It's just typical Chinglish."

◇

We were well beyond "Take Me Home, Country Roads." Other students had less interest in music, but opened up in other ways. Most of them were participating actively in class, engaged as thoughtfully as Isabel. Qing Fong, however, remained mute. Her writing was passionate, articulate, and unyielding. Each week she lasered in on me with her big brown eyes. But if I called on her, she merely shook her head. I would coax and cajole, but she remained stubborn and frosty. She had high cheekbones and hair pulled back in a bun. She kept her hands motionless on her desk for most of our classes, though on occasion she would pick up her pen without looking down and make a note or two. Her shirt was always starched and gleaming white, and her shoes were polished to a shine.

One day in November, during a five-minute break between the first and second hour of class, I approached Qing Fong to confront her about her silence. Before we could speak, however, Jennifer and Vivian popped into the classroom. They were whispering to each other as they sat down in the back of the room. I veered off from approaching Qing Fong and sat down next to my two smiling colleagues. I was relieved I had an excuse to avoid speaking with Qing Fong. There was a bit of Teacher Qing's tempting severity in her, as well as a bit of Kevin's formality. She unnerved me.

"I'm surprised to see you," I told Vivian and Jennifer.

"We heard good things about your class from Dean Wang," Vivian responded happily. "We hope we can sit in and join you."

Jennifer nodded in agreement. "We both have some free time," she added, "and this is a good way for us to practice our listening skills."

"But Jennifer," I teased, remembering her advice from earlier in the term, "I'm not asking students to repeat the experts. I'm asking them to be experts themselves."

She threw her hands up and opened her eyes wide. "I think I can handle it!" I nodded and welcomed them to the class. They would sit in for the rest of the year.

Break ended before I could return to Qing Fong and so I headed back to the front of the room and got our discussion going again. As often happens to me when a class goes well, I lost track of time, and before I knew it, students were packing up their things and heading out the door.

I realized with a shock that during that day's discussion of

Kurt Vonnegut I had completely forgotten I was in China. For more than an hour, I was totally unaware of where I was (or of place at all). It was the first time this had happened since I had exited the plane in Chengdu almost eighteen months prior. It was no small feat. There was, after all, always something to make me aware I was a stranger in a strange land, from the Chinese I heard around me, to the smell of stinky tofu, to the burn of pollution in my lungs, to the discomfort of mild diarrhea in my bowels. There were constant visceral reminders I was not in Kansas anymore. But in class with the postgraduates I felt like I was fully in my element and fully myself. I was not speaking English slowly. I was not self-censoring. I was in the zone, whatever that means.

I stood in silence as the students left the room. Isabel was the last to leave. She wore a leather jacket over a pastel sundress. "This was a wonderful class," she told me. I gave an aw-shucks smile. She went on to tell me that she and her classmates didn't agree on much, but one thing they all believed was that China needed free thinkers and open-minded citizens. She handed me a bag of apples and scurried out after her classmates. Five pounds of fruit and an hour of good discussion left me happy to be a teacher, thankful to be a Peace Corps volunteer, and full of energy for the rest of the semester.

二十一

Dog Meat King

The fall raced quickly into winter and the holiday season came to Guizhou. Jennifer's Yom Kippur fast went off without a hitch. Unlike her diet-clinic experience, she did not faint. "I also lost half a kilo," she told me, giving me a high five. If Yom Kippur was no more than a diet and a crucifix was nothing but a fashion accessory, perhaps Greg the Australian had been right. "They'll take what they need from you even if you don't want to give it," he had told me before biting open a beer. The rest, he insisted, would be rejected.

I hated to admit it, but Greg was onto something.

A collision of December holidays made this even more apparent. Hanukah, Christmas, and a local dog-eating festival came together in a few weeks of revel and song. An awkward conundrum thus confronted many upwardly mobile families for whom all things Western were symbols of status. They wanted to give Christmas gifts, and the gift of a puppy was the most genuinely foreign (and therefore meaningful) of all. But they also wanted to eat puppy. Could December 24th include a Christmas Eve dinner of poodle stew? And how would it feel to follow the stew with the gift of a Pekinese puppy? Isabel called this "a postmodern conundrum."

Jennifer agreed. "I'm not sure if we can combine our traditions with yours," she told me, "but I want it all." We celebrated an early Hanukah together by exchanging presents and heading to what she assured me was the best dog restaurant in town, the famous Dog Meat King. Jennifer was happy because a bid she had made on a condo in the center of town had been accepted, and the very next day a teacher in the Chinese department at Gui Da had asked her out on a date. "Once he found out I bought a home, he thought I was rich," she told me with a mischievous grin. "He is ugly, but I can accept him." She was positively glowing.

We sat at a tiny table in the back of a boisterous room and unwrapped our gifts. Jennifer gave me a pirated boxed set of *Lost* DVDs. I gave her a copy of a pirated version of *Harry Potter and the Half-Blood Prince*. This book, like other bits of intellectual property in China, was a mash-up hybrid of the genuine and the fake. At the end of the book Harry ended up not with Ginny Weasley but instead with the Chinese Hogwart's student, Cho Choi. This was one of dozens of alternate-ending Potter books for sale in China, each of which claimed to be the original work of J. K. Rowling. Jennifer told me this was, in fact, the real ending to the book. "Why wouldn't Harry choose the Chinese girl?" she asked earnestly. What was real? What was fake? It was another postmodern conundrum.

Jennifer tucked the book into her purse and yelled to the waiter. She was ready for business, quickly ordering our dinner. "Everyone wants to eat dog today," she explained as a stew was placed in front of me. "We believe that if you eat their meat on this day, you will stay warm all winter." My stew had beefy-looking cubes floating next to chunks of carrot and pepper. I eyed the cubes suspiciously.

I had resisted joining Jennifer at Dog Meat King for months. She was, as usual, relentless, and ever since our real estate outing she had been more insistent than ever that we eat together. "I must repay your kindness," she told me, "and can only do it by taking you to this flavorful restaurant. Plus, we must celebrate my new property and my new love!"

When I finally relented and agreed to go to Dog Meat King, I did so with no intention of eating the meat that gave the restaurant its name. I would sit with Jennifer, eat something innocuous, and finally get her off my back. Kosher, of course, had long ago gone out the window. But as I sat at the restaurant, hungry and happy to be with Jennifer, I felt a Moment of Truth emerging from a greasy haze.

Was I about to go fully native?

"Maybe there's no real difference between pig and dog," I thought to myself as I stared at the dish that sat between us on the table. I lifted a dog cube with my chopsticks and stared at it. The face of my brother's golden retriever, Eliot, appeared in the veins of the meat. He smiled at me and panted. I inhaled the fragrance and to my horror, my mouth began to water. Eliot disappeared. I closed my eyes and concentrated on Larry the Poodle, Lady and Loki the Terriers, Garp the Great Pyrenees, Monty the Border Collie, and all of the other dogs that had been underfoot when I was growing up. My mother—an animal lover to the core—made sure we never had fewer than two dogs at any one time, and rescues were ever present. I wanted to not want to eat this dog, but when I opened my eyes, the meat cube still seemed inviting.

Could I cross this culinary Rubicon? I thought of Greg the Australian once again, this time recalling his question about why I was in Guizhou. I had been unable to answer him with anything more than a quote from *Sang Doo, Let's Go to School!* Perhaps the whole purpose of this voyage was to try new things.

I opened my mouth, prepared to take a nibble, prepared to become fully integrated into life as a Peace Corps–Guizhou mutt.

This was the wrong metaphor to consider, and I hesitated. Can an American who eats dog ever be trusted? I was about to come as close to cannibalism as was legally possible. If I ate puppy and liked it, would I be unable to resist actual human flesh?

I licked the meat. The sky did not fall. I popped the cube into my mouth. I chewed. I swallowed.

It tasted like chicken.

Jennifer and I sat together for a long time after dinner. She smoked her Zhongnanhai brand cigarettes, I sipped my Pubu beers. She spent a long time telling me about her new boyfriend, Zhou Lingming. "Lingming means 'reputation' or 'good name,'" she explained. "So you can call him Good Name Zhou." I asked if she and Good Name had kissed. She threw a peanut at me. "I am not a terrible girl!" she replied. But she did smirk before telling me the "romance story of her very first kiss." In college she had a boyfriend, her one and only relationship before Good Name came along ten years later. "I loved that first boy, but he ran away with another girl, a married woman from Shenzhen. I have never seen him since." She shook her head in disgust. "Still, when he kissed me, I understood much more about the world. So he will always be my true love. I will also always hate him."

Jennifer's story was interrupted by her phone. She had a text message. "It's my new boyfriend," she said in a voice a few keys higher than usual. "He's coming to meet you."

"Why would he want to meet me?" I asked.

Jennifer made an inscrutable face. "Actually, I want you to meet him. I know you are frustrated sometimes when the students ask you for love advice, but I really trust you. I want to know if you approve." I nodded. Jennifer was right that I didn't like playing the part of the Hollywood romance master, but I knew Jennifer well enough to feel a little protective. I would give Good Name Zhou the once-over.

Soon enough, he arrived. Good Name was short and stocky and wore a blue pinstripe suit that appeared to be made out of nylon. He carried a man-purse, marking him as a somewhat fashion-sensitive man of business. This seemed to fit Jennifer's personality and I took it as a good sign. Good Name had a flat face and pockmarked skin. He wasn't the handsomest man around, but he had a thick head of hair and a strong jaw. He bounded towards me as soon as we made eye contact and gripped my hand lightly in a half shake, half caress. "Hello, Mike," he told me in a deep voice. "I am so happy to meet you."

Good Name sat down with us and yelled to a waitress to bring two more bottles of beer. He sat facing me, putting his back to Jennifer. When the beer arrived, he looked at it with horror and sent it back. "This is not cold enough!" he grunted. "Can't you see we are here with a foreign guest? And bring us Snow beer, not this Guizhou garbage." The waitress looked at him wearily and shuffled away. She soon replaced the two bottles of Pubu with a slightly more expensive brand, Snow. Good Name poured a pair of shots. We toasted and emptied our glasses.

"Ms. He told me I could be your friend," Good Name said as he poured two more shots. He was using Jennifer's family name, a cute touch. He wiped a bit of beer from his chin and clinked my glass again. "Maybe you can teach me English and I can teach you Chinese. *Ganbei!*"

I looked past Good Name and towards Jennifer. She shrugged at me. Good Name shimmied his body to block my view of his girlfriend. I downed my drink. "Let's toast again," he chirped. "Happiness every day!" he said in English as we drank.

"You are a good drinker," I told Good Name after we did another shot. I was sure this compliment would please him. "You are not squishy like mud."

He beamed at me. "You are flattering with me with local

phrases. But it is true that I like to drink. This is just a part of Chinese culture." He leaned in close, poured me another shot of beer, and put his hand on my thigh. "We have a phrase, *jiu hou tu zhen shuo*. Have you heard it?" I nodded. The phrase was the Chinese equivalent of *in vino veritas*: in wine there is truth.

"We Chinese cannot trust a person until we have been drunk with them," Good Name told me as he swirled beer in his glass. "It's only after much drinking that we can see each other's true minds."

I knew I was in for a long night.

◇

A few hours and many beers later, Jennifer, Good Name, and I went our separate ways. Good Name made sure he had my cell phone number before we left and promised to call me soon. He and Jennifer went off in opposite directions without a word or a glance. It was not a romance moment.

There had been little romance that evening, but there had been a number of surprises. I was surprised that dog meat tasted good. I was surprised that Jennifer had a boyfriend. The biggest surprise, however, was just around the corner, and I found it as I stumbled home. I had turned out of the alley that contained Dog Meat King and into a smaller, unlit crevice between two buildings, looking to relieve my bursting bladder. It was a quiet evening and few people were around, but I still wanted a bit of privacy. This was probably unnecessary since public urination was viewed much differently in Guiyang than it had been in Philadelphia. To categorize the two cities' attitudes about the act of peeing in public: Philly found it amusing; Guiyang saw it as a civic duty. In Guiyang, children usually wore crotchless and assless pants. "It is more convenient," Dean Wang had once told me when I reacted negatively to a child pausing, squatting, and pooping next to me. "Convenient for whom?" I replied.

Adults were not supposed to drop trou in the middle of the

sidewalk, but I could still pee on a building and not feel like a scofflaw. Still, the privacy helped, and I sighed with relief. After zipping up my fly and taking a moment to try to stop my head from spinning, I rounded the corner back into the main alley and had my biggest shock of the evening: I ran into Big Twin. In my bleary state I was at first unsure I was seeing clearly. What was she doing in an alley behind Gui Da at 11:00 p.m.?

I hadn't seen Big Twin in over a month. She was wearing a greasy apron, her hair hanging loosely in her face as she squatted over a basin full of dirty dishes. There was a sheen of sweat on her brow, her eyes were blank, and she scrubbed the dishes with purpose. I stood a few yards away from her, not sure if I should say hello. I didn't want to embarrass her by catching her doing this dirty work.

She spotted me before I could think my way through the situation, and greeted me with her usual smile. She jumped up. Would she feel ashamed of being covered in dirty water and working as a dishwasher? Her brow unfurled, and she squealed my name. A sparkle returned immediately to her eyes.

"I see you are working hard," I said to her awkwardly.

She nodded and pointed to an empty door frame behind her leading into a one-story brick building. "This is my uncle's restaurant. I've been working here for a few months now." The name of the restaurant hung on a hand-painted sign above the door frame: *Family Style*. It was, quite literally, a hole in the wall.

"It's a small place," I mumbled, half to myself, half to Big Twin. "How's the food?"

"Not bad," she said, with a genuine grin.

"But what about school?" I asked. Had I been sober, I'm sure I would have made an effort to be more tactful. *Jiu hou tu zhen shuo* was right.

"My father decided it is time for me to work." Big Twin was looking down as she spoke, but she was speaking with a confident voice. "Come inside and sit down. You're a little drunk. Let me make some food for you. I'm already a pretty good cook."

Big Twin led me through the door frame. The restaurant was a single white-tiled room. A bare lightbulb cast a flickering glow on the dirt floor. There were three plastic tables arranged in the center of the room, each with four small plastic stools tucked underneath. I stared at a cot in the corner of the room. "I can sleep there on nights when it is too late or too cold to go back home," Big Twin explained. "My uncle lets me sleep there for free."

Big Twin began humming and chopping vegetables. She moved the knife adeptly as if she had made this dish a thousand times before. Her hands were pink from burns and cracked from constant exposure to water. I felt nauseous. I couldn't tell how much of this feeling was coming from the beer sloshing around in my stomach and how much was coming from seeing Big Twin's new life.

"Is your little sister still in school?" I asked, though I was pretty sure I already knew the answer.

"No, she is working, too," Big Twin answered. She confirmed my sinking feeling that I had, indeed, seen Little Twin scavenging for recyclables in the center of Guiyang. Each discarded can of Coke or empty water bottle she managed to wrestle away from the other kids roaming the streets could be redeemed for one-tenth of a penny. I knew this was a common job for Bouyei girls. As bad as Big Twin's job seemed, her sister's was far worse.

I blurted out a question I knew might be inappropriate: "Aren't you both too young to be working?"

Big Twin paused her chopping and looked at me evenly. "Our family must support my oldest sister." I had never met the oldest Wang, but I knew she was studying chemistry at a nearby college. She had scored high enough on the *Gao Kao* to have a chance to escape life in the village. If she was really lucky, she would leave Guizhou altogether and get a job on the coast. This would allow her to send a good bit of money back to the family in China's internal remittance system. The Wang family was making a rational economic decision to educate the one daughter who could, in essence, repay the money spent on tuition.

"What is Wang Number One doing?" I asked.

"She will finish middle school," Big Twin responded. "I don't know why she gets to have this chance, but I will do whatever needs to be done to support her and my oldest sister." She returned to her chopping. "The rest of the family must sacrifice. This is Chinese culture."

"How does Little Twin feel about working?"

Big Twin shook her head and placed a bowl of soup in front of me. "She is not happy. She refuses to come home. She believes that in a new socialist economic system, all children must have basic knowledge to succeed." Big Twin's words came right out of a government slogan. Unfortunately, the slogan was not yet matched by a government commitment to pay school fees. In rural Guizhou, there was no such thing as fully public education. "Our father can't afford the school fees. I support his decision, but she hates him now."

"Why do you work here, while she works with the water bottles?" I didn't know how to say 'recycling,' but Big Twin understood what I was getting at.

"I learned simple math, so I can work with money in a restaurant. My little sister is doing the only job she can do."

I drank my soup, my heart breaking with each sip. Big Twin's final year of middle school would have cost the equivalent of twenty-five dollars.

二十二

Friendship Jew

For the next few days I avoided going anywhere near the alley that contained Dog Meat King and Family Style. I wanted to avoid feeling guilty about eating dog meat, and I wanted to dodge the clichéd shame that came from comparing my life as a typical American to the life of a little girl from the Chinese countryside. I tried to put thoughts of animal cruelty and poverty out of my mind, or at least to contain them in tolerable categories.

Unfortunately, Australian Greg kept popping into my mind. Perhaps he was right about being a PCV in China. What good was I really doing? What good could any foreigner do? I felt guiltier and guiltier.

Guilt is, of course, a Jewish hobby. My mother is a connoisseur of the feeling and she taught me to savor it in all varieties. My grandmother had an even more sophisticated palate and was the family sommelier; she could match any situation to an appropriate bottle of soul-crushing self-loathing. Generations of preparation in the subtleties and varieties of guilt still left me unprepared for Guilt with Chinese Characteristics. I woke up three mornings in a row feeling like a rock had been placed on my chest. I also felt pain in my bowels. The former feeling was an existential crisis. The latter was *Giardia*. Big Twin's soup gave me a raging bout of this unpleasant infection.

I was able to kick the *Giardia* with a simple pill. The guilt was more troublesome. I tried to think of ways to channel my feelings into action, but nothing meaningful came to mind. I realized I would settle for mere distraction.

Salvation came in a call from Coach Qin. "I know you are busy with the Christmas week," he told me, "but today we have a basketball clinic for some young students. Can you help?" I didn't know exactly what I was getting myself into, but I told Coach I was available. Anything was preferable to sitting and thinking impotently about the Wangs.

Coach showed up at my apartment a few minutes later in his Ford Focus. "Let's go," he said simply. Coach was in a good mood as we drove the same road we had taken during my recruitment trip six months earlier. (Had it really only been six months earlier? It felt like *years* had passed.) We were once again on the road to Qingyan Ancient Village. The road was in a state of disrepair, having been torn up by an army of construction workers. Hundreds of them had moved along miles of road with hammer and chisel in hand, many working barefoot and shirtless. The Guiyang government was planning on expanding the road to Qingyan to increase tourism. For the time being, we had to drive over rocks and around massive potholes.

Coach was happy because our team was on a long win streak. I had been playing well but was far from the only reason we were successful. Ah Ge, our point guard and captain, was a relentless defender and wasn't turning the ball over. Da Bao was rebounding and working hard to get up and down the court, despite being as fat as a dumpling. Shui, our center, was one of the better big men in the league. As a foreigner, I was afforded a status in the friendship-first hierarchy that was above the typical player, though below Communist Party members. In other words, white privilege went far in Guiyang, though not as far as party privilege. Still, more often than not, calls went my way and I was living at the free-throw line. Each free shot gave me a chance to ponder the social, political, and ethnic ranking system in Guiyang. At times, its strict enforcement meant I got banned from basketball games. At other times, it meant I got two free shots for mostly imaginary fouls.

On the strength of my teammates and my free-throw shooting, we won our games. Each win brought our team closer together. My teammates had even begun debating how to nickname me. Ah Ge wanted to call me *Bai Gui*, the White Ghost. Coach Qin wanted to call me *Feichung Fejii*, the Flying Philadelphian. Shui, however, got the most support when he suggested *You Qing You Tai*, or Friendship Jew.

I didn't care what the team called me. I was just happy to have a way to relax and to get my mind off the more depressing aspects of life in Guiyang. Coach saw I was feeling down and asked what was wrong. I told him about the Wang twins. His response to my story was a bit cryptic though it somehow put me a bit more at ease. "You cannot change the course of a river," he told me. "But you can learn to appreciate its beauty and power."

"That's true," I responded as our car lurched over a particularly egregious sinkhole. "But not all rivers are beautiful. I can't find any silver lining in Guiyang's poverty."

Coach nodded and held my hand. "You are a good teacher, Mike, and a good basketball player, and you have some new friends. This is all we can control in this world."

◇

We soon arrived at Qingyan Ancient Village. The rest of the team was waiting at the entrance to the town. Coach and I joined them and we all approached the gate together. Once again, there was no fee. Coach simply slapped the guard on the back and gave him a cigarette. *Guanxi* was a wonderful thing.

We followed Coach through the narrow streets. This visit,

unlike my first, took place during normal business hours, and there was a happy bustle all around me. There were Miao women selling silver jewelry, Bouyei families beckoning to me to look at their handwoven clothing, and adorable little shops selling candy and wine. My teammates were poking in and out of stores as we walked, hanging on each other, flirting with cute girls, and bargaining for knickknacks. I was looking at an ivory mahjong set when Ah Ge called out to me. He was inside a wine store across the alley.

"Let's have a quick drink," he yelled over to me.

I put down the mahjong set and hopped across the alley. Ah Ge grabbed me around the waist and led me into the wine store. It had about a dozen huge clay jars, each with a handwritten sign hanging from the neck. "Rose Wine," said one. "Hibiscus Wine," said another.

"What kind do you want to try?" asked the store owner, a middle-aged man with tanned skin. "It's all delicious, and I offer very good prices."

Ah Ge asked for a bit of the rose wine. The owner opened the jar, reached inside with a wooden cup, and pulled out a small bit of the pink liquid. Ah Ge took a sip and frowned. "It's not very sweet," he said. The owner clicked his tongue and pursed his lips. He took a sip as well. "It's delicious!" he retorted. "But if you don't like it, you can try another. I'm sure you'll find something you like."

I saw a few wines with names I could not understand. "Does that say lizard wine?" I asked, pointing to a jar towards the back of the store. Ah Ge nodded. "Yes," he told me. "There are different things you can put in wine to make it more potent."

"That wine is very good for your *qi*," the owner added, rushing over to get a spoonful. "It helps balance the hot and cold in your body." I followed him and looked inside the jar. Sure enough, visible through the clear wine were a dozen or so dead lizards, each about eight inches long. I sipped from the spoon. It tasted no different from other rice wines, but I suppose my lizard palate was unrefined.

"I don't like it," I told him. "What about this one?" I said pointing to a jar with the characters 鹿 鞭 酒 or, from what I could understand, "deer whip wine." "What's a deer whip?" The owner and Ah Ge laughed together. Ah Ge put his finger down near his crotch and thrust his hips. He said a single word in English: "Cock!"

"Inside of this jar I have many deer penises," the owner told me with wide eyes. "And not just any deer, but Tibetan deer. This will make you a better man in bed." The owner was fishing inside the jar for a bit of wine for me to taste. I peered inside the jar but the liquid inside was too dark to allow me to see any deer genitals. "It's a little bit expensive," the owner said as I sipped, "but I can give you a discount." Before I could say a word, Ah Ge and the owner were negotiating. We ended up with a pint of deer cock wine. Remarkably, the wine didn't even strike me as odd. All prudishness about food and drink were long gone.

While the thought of drinking the wine gave me no pause, it did remind me of the ever-present conflict between my desire to maintain a sense of self and the Peace Corps ideal of immersion. Where was the line between a serious moral mistake and the breach of a mere cultural taboo? How far should I flex as a guest? When was it OK to pass judgment? I would never go native enough to punch a bag full of puppies, but it seemed I would eat and drink anything put in front of me on a plate, in a bowl, or filling a cup. When it came to animals, I had apparently established a rule: if it was dead, I would eat it; if it was alive, I would protect it. I wasn't sure if this made any sense.

One thing I *was* sure of was how far I had come since leaving Philadelphia. Boarding the plane for China marked the end of a long run of vegetarianism. In college, I cut meat out of my diet, out of fear that I was contributing to the suffering of animals. I went deep into the animal-rights movement, evangelizing to any of my American friends who loved a good barbeque. For ten years, I tormented my family with stories of factory farms, tortured little veal calves, and sad chickens. I saw nothing but hypocrisy in a nation of dog-owning sausage eaters. I never went completely over the deep end: I never swept through the South Street Diner grabbing fistfuls of bacon while shouting slogans about porcine liberation. But perhaps this was exactly how my puppy intervention appeared to the passengers on the bus who watched me fight with the dog abusers.

I didn't have any answers. I would simply have to continue muddling through, confronting what I perceived as egregious acts of animal cruelty—however ineffectively—while also enjoying wines created through what could only have been a miserable moment for a Tibetan deer.

◇

Ah Ge and I emerged from the wine shop and hustled to catch up with the team. They were already on a side path that ran up a hill towards the heart of Qingyan. At the top of the hill was a tiny Buddhist temple. It was the main attraction of the village, reconstructed to look like the original temple which had stood for hundreds of years before being torn down during the Cultural Revolution. The temple had a few shrines, a small vegetarian restaurant, a dormitory for the monks, and an open courtyard full of well-tended plants. The courtyard also had a basketball hoop.

"We will be teaching some orphans how to play basketball," Coach explained to me as we walked the last fifty yards up the hill. "I'm sure these poor children have never seen a foreigner in person, so you will be very popular today." He took a long drag from his cigarette as we arrived at the gate to the temple.

Three dozen kids were waiting for us. They ranged from toddlers to middle-school-aged. A monk stood in the courtyard in front of the children. He had a shaved head and wore saffron robes. His feet were covered in rope sandals. Coach Qin walked up to him and they greeted each other warmly.

"Welcome to Qingyan," the monk said to the team. "The children are very excited to play with you." The kids were standing at attention, but upon seeing us they came near to bursting with excitement. They strained to stand in the positions they had obviously been told to maintain. Their feet stayed glued in place, but they leaned into one another and whispered behind hands. A few were shaking and dancing in place, unable to contain their energy. As our team lined up in front of them, they started cheering and a few jumped up and down. Each wore a red handkerchief around his or her neck. I had recently learned this was a sign of membership in the Young Pioneers, a sort of Boy Scout / Communist-in-Training club.

I took a moment to soak in my surroundings. From high up on this hill I could see down into the winding alleys of Qingyan. It was a lot bigger than I thought and stretched far in each direction. To the east, the village ran all the way to the Huaxi River. I looked again at the children. The boys each had short haircuts, threadbare pants and jackets, and cheap plastic sandals. The girls had their hair tied in ponytails and wore school uniforms— jumpsuits much like those worn by Big and Little Twin when they had been in school. My mind wandered back to the first picnic I had with the Wang girls. I thought of tree climbing, singing, and laughter.

A grunt from the monk called me back from my daydream. The monk's *hut!* sound also snapped the children to attention.

"This is a group that has come from Guizhou University to teach you today," he said in a surprisingly stern tone. His voice was loud and crisp. "You will learn some basic physical knowledge from them, so pay careful attention." The monk called one of the boys forward. He looked at us nervously before introducing himself.

"I am the class monitor," he told us stiffly. He stood tall and kept hands thrust down at his sides. This was a future Kevin Chen. "We have prepared a performance for you. Please enjoy it." He turned and directed the students to positions around the courtyard. They quickly scattered into a semicircle and, after a short pause, started singing. Their song had a sweet melody, half lullaby, half folk song. It was a tune I recognized, about a boy and a girl falling in love in the moonlight. *"First, he loves her because he knows she is pretty,"* they sang. *"Second, because she knows how to care for a family."*

Along with the singing, the girls soon marched into the center of the semicircle and performed a choreographed dance. They bowed to the boys and swept their hands over their heads. The dance was slow and hypnotic. It ended with all of the girls curled up in little balls on the ground.

Coach Qin and the team gave the kids a big round of applause. I joined them, following their lead and wondering what was next. "Thank you for your song," said Coach Qin. "We can return one for you, to show our friendship." The team suddenly looked at me. Coach gave me a mysterious smile. "I think you should sing for them," he told me in English. "Don't be nervous. They are just children, after all."

I was happy to oblige. I stepped forward and sang "I'm a Little Teapot." After the first verse, the orphans were smiling and doe-eyed. After the second, they were clapping and shaking with delight. After the third, they were frothing at the mouth, crazed with teapot fervor. Based on their reactions, I felt—with all modesty—that I was offering the greatest rendition of "I'm a Little Tea Pot" in human history. I hammed up my dancing, sang loud, and looked at each of the kids. One of the little boys was so excited to see this performance that he was laughing and weeping. Tears streamed down his face, washing away the dirt on his cheeks.

Friendship Jew had done it again.

We spent the afternoon singing with the kids and eventually

running them through some basketball drills. It was a bit chaotic and hilariously fun. Ah Ge was a natural with kids and they ended up chasing him around asking for piggyback rides. They were thrilled to hear me sing in English and, naturally, got a kick out of the hair on my arms, the size of my nose, and the goofy way I spoke Chinese.

By the end of our games, I was exhausted and famished. We all had dinner together in the restaurant next door. I stuffed myself full of tofu and eggplant. The kids ate bowl after bowl of rice. My teammates yawned and smoked cigarettes. We all had a shot of deer cock wine.

"This seems to have cheered you up," Coach Qin told me.

I nodded. "I am really grateful to be on your team," I told him. "This was an awesome day."

He winked at me and snuffed out his cigarette. I looked down again to the Huaxi River in the distance. It meandered from Qingyan all the way past the Wang village and into the center of Guiyang. It passed within a few hundred yards of Gui Da, my apartment, and the Walmart. It was full of oil slicks and garbage. Still, from my angle, high above, it looked beautiful.

二十三

That's Not Jesus

With Christmas only a few days away, my office hours were more frantic than usual. Students were excited for another round of the ultimate Western holiday. Isabel, who had distinguished herself as my top graduate student, brought me a Santa hat with a white beard attached. She covered her mouth and laughed as I put it on. "Santa has come to China!" she told the others in the office. On that particular day, Isabel had Qing Fong in tow. They were holding hands when they entered the office and they chatted quietly while I was busy with other students. I had still failed to penetrate the veil of silence Qing Fong had wrapped around herself. Her writing was always lovely, but she did not have the confidence to speak. She greeted me with a nod that day and, as always, stayed silent and intensely alert. The way she stared at me was always a little unnerving, teetering between attentive and obsessive. I was convinced that I had never seen her blink.

When the undergraduate students left the office and headed to class, I removed the Santa beard and told Isabel I was glad to see her. "I've got something I've wanted to ask you about," I told her, before describing the Wang family. I was interested in hearing the reflections of a woman from China's wealthy coast.

Would she want to help the girls? Would she agree with Dean Wang's belief that the Bouyei were primitive? Would she respond with *meibanfa*, the often-used summary of hopelessness?

At thirty years old, Isabel was the oldest woman I taught (setting aside my auditors, Vivian and Jennifer). She was also one of my few Chinese friends who was married, though her husband, Handsome, was living back in Shanghai. They would spend three years more than a thousand miles apart. If Vivian and Isabel were any indication, long-distance marriage was nothing out of the ordinary for young Chinese. Isabel was looking forward to reuniting with her spouse. She would blush whenever she spoke of Handsome, and I got the impression that they were deeply in love.

"If I am very lucky, my Master's thesis will be accepted by Professor Fei this spring so I can head home," she told me. "I didn't even want to come to Guizhou University, but my school back home forced me to accept this place so they could develop *guanxi*. I hoped Professor Fei would read my thesis last year, but he went to Sichuan University, so I had to wait another year to graduate."

Isabel's thesis compared Emily Brontë with Zhu Shaolin, a contemporary Chinese author. Both women wrote at first under androgynous pen names. Both were more realist than romantic. Isabel explained to me that Zhu's novel *A Song of the Sad Coffee Shop* had the same tone as *Wuthering Heights*. She spoke of both books with passion. I hoped Professor Fei would approve the thesis so that Isabel could get home to Handsome.

"When Handsome and I have a child," she told me, "we will provide an education." She had listened closely to my description of the Wang family and the father's decision to pull the girls from school. "But what else can your friend, Mr. Wang, possibly do?" Isabel frowned. "Sometimes I wish life was simple, like it was for my parents. In those days, there was purpose. There was a guide in Chairman Mao. Now, China has no guide. We have nothing but confusion. The traditional values are all invisible. The poor people here in Guiyang can only struggle."

At this, Qing Fong cleared her throat. I looked at her and leaned forward in my seat. Would I finally hear her voice? She took a deep breath and spoke: "Isabel is right," she mumbled quietly. "The difference between Guiyang, my hometown, and Shanghai, Isabel's hometown, is like the difference between a chicken and a hawk. Guiyang will never be able to fly and never be able to compete."

Isabel looked at her friend sadly. "It will be difficult for Qing Fong to ever escape," she said to no one in particular.

Qing Fong agreed. "Things are rarely fair in life. But I have promised to devote myself to making China a better place." Her gaze became, if possible, even more intense. "I have wondered about your intentions, Mike. But I think perhaps I can trust you."

As Qing Fong spoke, a pencil-thin student wearing blue jeans and a rugby jumper opened my door. I had seen her on campus and knew she was an English major, but I had never met her. I smiled at her and she stepped tentatively over the threshold and walked towards me. She extended her hand, blushed violently, and introduced herself as Ragamuffin. Her hair hid much of her face and she spoke quietly.

"My father works for the government," she mumbled, "and he heard there was a foreign teacher in Guiyang. He wants to have a relationship with you."

"Hmmm," I mumbled. I looked at Isabel, who had pursed her lips. Qing Fong was, for the first time, smiling. "Hmmm," I repeated.

Eventually, I expressed myself in words. "What kind of relationship does your father want with me?"

"He wants to create an authentic Christmas celebration. He says you will guide him."

Relieved, I told Ragamuffin I would be happy to help, but admitted I was not the most qualified guide into the world of

Hosannas. "I don't celebrate Christmas," I explained, tucking my Santa beard into a desk drawer. "I'm no expert."

Ragamuffin was confused: "I thought you are an American."

"I am," I replied. "But I am Jewish. We don't celebrate Christmas."

These words did not faze Ragamuffin. "Americans celebrate Christmas," she said with conviction.

"I'd be happy to help you have an authentic Hanukah celebration," I offered, in what I thought was a reasonable compromise.

"What is Hanukah?"

"It's the Festival of Lights!"

"That is not America. Tell me about the American holiday of Christmas. Tell me what is authentic."

I shrugged and did my best. I described pine trees with angels on top, elves and reindeer, green and red wrapping paper, and the yearly ritual of spending Christmas Eve in a Chinese restaurant.

This startled Ragamuffin. "Americans eat Chinese food on Christmas?"

"Well, *Jewish* Americans certainly do." I emphasized the Jewish.

"Is that because Comrade Marx was Jewish, and China upholds his beliefs?"

"No," I said, smiling at her answer. "It's because everything else is closed."

Our conversation continued for a few minutes, and at some point during the back-and-forth, I agreed to meet her father. The meeting had, in typical Guiyang fashion, already been planned—my "decision" to agree was assumed.

◇

The next afternoon, a car was sent for me, and soon Mr. Ragamuffin and I sat drinking beer in a bar in downtown Guiyang.

The bar was called South Park, named by its owner for the American cartoon. It had a wide variety of fake American booze; Ragamuffin's dad wisely chose something local.

"*Ganbei*," he said, tipping back a glass of Pubu. He wore a light-grey suit and had short-cropped hair. His thick local accent made him difficult for me to understand, but he spoke slowly and had a kind voice. He ordered us some food, more beer, and told me his plans.

Mr. Ragamuffin had used his position in the Communist Party to get a managerial job at the Guiyang Walmart. "I want to be a good manager and move up in the company," he told me. He had recently come up with an idea: he wanted a genuine Santa to be present, a Santa who would induce an American-style buying orgy. "Christmas is about buying," he told me confidently, "but Guiyang people are too primitive to understand this yet. Christianity will teach them how to buy."

Mr. Ragamuffin had an addition to his pitch. "This can help build profound international relationships." I liked the phrase. I agreed to help. "Be at the Walmart tomorrow night for Christmas Eve. Everything has been prepared in advance."

◇

Mr. Ragamuffin sent another car to pick me up at Gui Da the next day. I rode along Huaxi highway as my driver smoked cigarette after cigarette. Traffic was bad, so the ride took over an hour. I was glad to be in the front seat of a Buick rather than crammed onto a bus. "How many more times will I ride this highway?" I thought to myself. Everything I had experienced in my first eighteen months in China was new and imbued with meaning. Everything I was experiencing in this final lap was, potentially, a Last Time. This was my Last Christmas. I would soon give my Last Exam. I would go through my Last Spring Festival. Eventually, I would play in my Last Basketball Game. I tried to banish these thoughts from my mind. The view outside the car helped distract me.

Pictures of Santa Claus had been hung throughout the city. I saw dozens in shop windows along the highway. There were also life-sized Santa blow-up dolls on the tops of apartment buildings, and people wandering around in fake white beards. I knew young people in Guiyang loved to imitate the West. There were days when I felt I was living in a simulacrum, or at least a parody, of life back home. LeBron James was on billboards. Céline Dion was on the radio. Santa was suddenly ubiquitous.

Any questions I had about the Santa invasion would be answered by Kevin Chen, class monitor and PLA poster boy. He surprised me by opening my door as the car pulled into the Walmart parking lot. Kevin explained that Mr. Ragamuffin had hired him as protection.

"Protection?" I said. "Protection from what?"

Kevin pointed to a crowd of a few hundred people milling about near the entrance to the Walmart. "Santa has made them excited," he told me. "They might not understand how to treat you." Kevin wore flip-flops and a Kobe Bryant jersey. He did not look like he was ready to rumble.

I was unnerved. Before I could ask if Kevin was secretly armed, or if there were other bodyguards to help protect me, I was hustled into the Louvre Pyramid and quickly whisked down the escalator into the Walmart. Someone in the crowd saw me and shouted, "Foreigner!" Others pointed and cried out. "It's Santa!" said some. "It's Jesus!" yelled at least one other. The crowd rushed after us, pouring down the escalator in a dangerous avalanche. Kevin ran me into a tiny back office and slammed the door shut, locking it behind us.

"We will wait here until the crowd has calmed down. Then it will be your time. They are all waiting for Santa Claus." Kevin handed me a plastic bag containing my costume for the evening. I could hear the crowd outside shouting and chanting. I slowly put on my red pants, white beard, and floppy hat. Rushing down the escalator, I had felt like a movie star running from paparazzi. I now felt like a rodeo clown or a member of a bomb squad.

After about an hour, when the cries from the crowd had disappeared, I peered out of the office and saw that the mob had been pushed back; security guards had them hemmed behind a rope. "Kevin," I said, "I'm usually pretty flexible, and I don't mind not knowing exactly what's going on." I wiped sweat from my forehead. "But this seems more absurd than usual. What should I do out there?"

"Run around the store and scream at people," Kevin told me. "Scream at them to buy."

I laughed nervously. Seemed easy enough. It was a bit like Dean Wang's initial advice to me about how to teach. "Get them to open their mouths," he had said. I succeeded then, so why not now?

"Your time has come," Kevin told me. He handed me a can of Silly String and a rubber mallet. "These are your tools. Good luck." Kevin threw open the door and pushed me out. The crowd went momentarily silent before erupting and rolling over the security guards and their rope. I screamed and ran down the electronics aisle, shooting Silly String over my shoulder.

For the next two hours, I sprinted around Walmart, sometimes chasing delighted shoppers, sometimes being chased by them. They, too, were armed with Silly String and mallets, accessories that apparently are to Guiyang Christmas what mistletoe is to American Christmas (or would be if mistletoe could be weaponized). It was at first a terrifying experience, but the chase soon morphed into a sweaty, unthreatening blur. It was certainly not a typical Christmas. It was more like Mardi Gras. Either way, I'm certain I was the best Jewish Santa in Guiyang history.

◇

At the end of the night Kevin took me back into the little office, locked the door once again, and gave me a pat on the back. "That was a marvelous performance." He handed me a bottle of water which I downed in one long gulp. I peeled off the sweat-drenched Santa costume and flopped down on an old couch. My graceless collapse caused a stack of files on the far end of the couch to teeter, and Kevin sprang to catch them before they fell. After stabilizing the pile, he joined me on the couch.

"Your Santa performance inspired me," Kevin said with awe in his voice. "I am a confident boy, but I would never be able to do something like that. I think Americans are more outgoing than Chinese."

"Some are," I replied. "Some aren't."

Kevin bounced back up off the couch and walked to the far corner of the office. He squatted down in front of a low refrigerator. It looked like the sort of mini-fridge you would find in a hotel or a college dorm room. He opened it up and pulled out two ice-cold cans of Budweiser. "These are imported," he told me. "I think since you are in Walmart, you should take advantage of products from your home." My mouth immediately felt like it was full of cotton and sand that only a Bud could wash away. Kevin tossed me a can. I cracked it open and as the seal hissed I imagined a beer commercial crossing from television into my life. Twelve coeds poured into the office, all wearing skimpy elf costumes. Santa and Kevin exchanged the "Oh yeah!" look of the dim-witted but lucky.

Or so I imagined. No blondes appeared, but the beer was still delicious. Kevin seemed to be enjoying his as well. He kept taking sips and then looking at the can. "America is much different in our textbooks," he stated evenly.

"I've told you what I think of your textbooks," I replied.

Kevin ignored me. "Our texts tell us Americans, who have empty capitalism, suffer from a profound malaise, called the American Malaise. They tell us you cannot find any reason to live other than money or false religion. It is said that the profound malaise widely spreads."

I groaned and buried my head in my hands. "I hope you don't take that too seriously," I told him.

He tilted his head to the side. "I think I used to. But now that I've become your friend, I can't believe it. You are the happiest person I have ever met." Kevin finished off his beer.

I thought about Kevin's observation for a few moments. "I guess I've just got a lot to be thankful for." He nodded and returned to the fridge, snagging two more cans of beer. He cracked both open, handing one to me and again looking at his own. He seemed to be looking for a secret message inscribed on the aluminum.

We sat in that cramped office for a long time. It was a welcome reprieve from the insanity of the Santa chase. The Walmart slowly closed around us, eventually slipping into a cryptlike silence and darkness. By midnight, we were alone in the bowels of Guiyang, deep below the People's Park. We finished off the six-pack while chatting away. Kevin told me that his classes bored him, but he studied hard anyway since he wanted to go to graduate school. He was obviously a motivated young man but our conversation made it clear that he had no direction in life. He explained to me that he didn't know if he should pursue money, political purity, love, or tradition. He wasn't as poor as the Wang girls, but he—like Qing Fong—didn't have much of a shot at getting to the coast. Isabel would head back to Shanghai. Vivian would get to Beijing through marriage. Kevin was not so lucky, and despite his leadership roles, his strong English skills, and his raw intelligence, he felt he had no hope of finding a job he would enjoy.

"Perhaps I'm the one with profound malaise," he told me with a crooked smile. "Could you offer me some advice? What do you think I should pursue in my life?"

I broke some bad news to Kevin: "I'm just an English teacher. I can't really offer you much guidance. I think I should stick to grammar and vocabulary."

"But tonight you were Santa," Kevin retorted.

He had me there. I was more than a walking, talking diction-ary and grammar machine. At the very least, I was a symbol of something. But what was it? Kevin and I pondered in silence. Eventually, I did all that I could think to do: I invited him to join my postmodern literature class. It would, at least, get him away from his awful texts and mind-numbing undergraduate classes. Maybe what Kevin was looking for was a chance to think freely. He gratefully accepted my offer and promised to join us after winter vacation. There were only half a dozen meetings planned for the spring term, but I thought Kevin could still learn a lot from Isabel, Qing Fong, and the other postgraduate students.

"Did you know," Kevin told me as we finished the last beers, "that there is a Jewish book that can help people with all of their problems? It is the best-selling book in China right now." The book, which I later found out was called *Jewish People's Secrets for Success*, was, indeed, a hot seller. It had been written by a former factory worker from Guangdong. The book had a pic-ture of a dollar-covered Torah on the cover, and snapshots of Marx, Einstein, Vladimir Putin, and Bill Gates on the back. "The author will become bigger than even Li Yang," Kevin said to me that night in the office, referring to the cult leader of the Crazy English! training school.

"That wouldn't surprise me," I told him as we shut off the lights and prepared to leave. It was eerie to be in such a large store with no one else around. Our steps echoed as we walked up the dormant escalator.

"Do you have any real Jewish secrets?" Kevin asked. I didn't bother to answer, and Kevin laughed at his own question. "I can't even believe I said that," he concluded. "I guess I'm just a little desperate. I wish I could find a new direction in my life."

For some reason, Coach Qin jumped to mind. "You cannot change the course of a river," I told Kevin. "But you can learn to appreciate its beauty and power."

He paused and looked at me. "I've heard that somewhere before. Is it from the Bible?"

I shook my head. "I don't think so. It's something my coach told me."

Kevin cut me off with an "Aha!" We had reached the top of the escalator and emerged into the cool night air. "That's a translation of a Li Yuchun lyric," he told me, referring to the winner of the previous year's *Super Girl* competition.

Kevin had closed his eyes tightly. "I'm trying to translate the next line for you . . ." We were walking in the People's Park towards the Mao statue. Kevin soon opened his eyes and started singing. *"I am difficult to love,"* he warbled, *"but I can be your power woman."* He hit a high falsetto with the last two words and repeated them, drawing them out. *"Power wommmmmaaaaan!"*

Coach Qin had given me advice sung to him by a nineteen-year-old girl. I had taken it to heart and passed it along. Truth can always be found in a good love ballad.

二十四

Pop That Pussy

I couldn't help Kevin with the Malaise, and neither could Li Yuchun. I did, however, find an opportunity to help the Wang family. It fell right in my lap: in late January, President Bill asked me to judge the Guiyang City Spring Festival English Singing Contest. The winner would walk away with a hundred-dollar grand prize. I knew that a bit of money was not a solution to the Wangs' problems; it would be but a salve for a symptom of a systemic problem. Still, a quick fix felt better than nothing. I shoehorned Big Twin's name onto the list of contestants.

Li Mei had warned me to "beware of overinvolvement." Perhaps her advice, like Coach Qin's wisdom, was of the pop variety. Perhaps she had read her line in a fortune cookie. Either way, I was willing to take a risk.

The contest was held on a cool evening in the city's fanciest hotel, the Sheng Feng Inn. I was one of four judges and the only foreigner. We sat in the front row of a large, well-appointed conference room and were introduced, one by one, to a packed house. The audience was in a festive mood and energy was high. Spring Festival had already passed, but the late singing contest gave everyone a reason to do a bit of drinking. A good portion of the room seemed to be rip-roaring drunk.

There were ten contestants on the list, and each had chosen an English song to perform, karaoke style. Big Twin—who had instantly agreed to sing in the contest when I let her know she had the chance—was prepared to sing the crowd-pleasing Céline Dion hit "My Heart Will Go On." I wasn't sure what the other contestants had prepared, but I knew Big Twin would at least be competitive. She had a sweet, pure voice, an irresistible smile, and loved to perform. I gave her good odds.

Before the competition began, President Bill—the MC for the night—handed me a pamphlet, translated into English for my benefit, explaining how the competition would be judged. The pamphlet told me that I should give each contestant a score out of a hundred, "based equally on singing skills, performance on the stage, pronunciation, and positivity." I was unclear how to judge someone's "positivity" so I asked the judge to my left, a handsome old man in white leather shoes, for clarification. He responded in English: "That means the song should have good value for the student's political learning."

I nodded knowingly. "I see." But I didn't see: "So the song should promote Communism?"

The man smiled. "Something like that."

The singing contest opened with two warm-up acts. First, a gaggle of young men sang an a cappella version of Elton John's "Rocket Man." I was always a little surprised by which foreign songs had found their way into Chinese culture. Radiohead's relative absence made sense; they may have been one of the most popular bands in the world, but their songs weren't exactly melodic. But I still couldn't figure out why hair bands weren't bigger. I remained convinced that with a bit of exposure, Aerosmith, Van Halen, or Bon Jovi could light the province on fire. Guiyang was a dry heap of tinder; "Wanted Dead or Alive" was the match. Unfortunately, with only a few months left in China,

I wouldn't have time to melt the province's collective face with a Richie Sambora solo.

Meanwhile, young people on the cutting edge were starting to listen to hip-hop and heavy metal. Linkin Park was an underground sensation as was Kanye West. Still, the follow-up to "Rocket Man" jarred me: five skinny, scantily clad girls shimmied vigorously to "Pop That Pussy" by the ribald '80s rap group 2 Live Crew. I have no idea how or why they chose this particular song, but the other judges seemed happy to bob their heads as the students gyrated, the bass bumped, and the speakers boomed. The crowd, too, was enjoying the show as the young women lip-synched to the lyrics. I cringed as the words "champagne glass" were combined in a rhyme that ended in "stick my dick in your ass."

Clever, to be sure, but I was nonetheless mortified. I had, after all, invited a twelve-year-old girl to the competition. I scanned the room looking for Big Twin. I didn't spot her.

More rap music followed as the singing contest officially began. The crowd was drinking, shouting, hooting, and hollering. The first two contestants performed songs from the band of the moment, the Black Eyed Peas, known in China as *Hei Yan Dou Dou*. The band was popular in large part because two of its members looked vaguely Chinese—Taboo, a DJ, is half Mexican–half Native American; apl.de.ap, a rapper, is half Filipino. My students insisted that both were 100 percent Chinese.

The first contestant of the night was a young woman who had chosen the English name Lemonade. She chose to perform a hyperactive version of "Wo De Dian Fung" ("My Humps"). She shimmied across the stage while singing about her lovely lady humps.

I looked at my scorecard. "Singing skills, performance on the stage, pronunciation, and positivity." How to judge Lemonade? How, in particular, to score her "positivity"? Perhaps the song had some connection to Communism, though I couldn't find it. Could her "hump" be her passion for Chairman Mao? It was too much of a stretch. Total score: 62.

The next contestant, who went by the name Barry, was a lot better. He chose "Where Is the Love?" and, with his Yankees cap pulled low over his eyes, brought the ruckus, rapping about racism and the injustices of life in the American hood. He rapped quickly, and had the crowd hopping up and down in delight. More importantly for his score, his song bashed America and therefore had clear "positivity." Overall score: 86.

Next up, to my surprise, was Yvette Chen, student leader of the Guj. The club hadn't met in months. Jennifer had been too busy with Good Name to organize any events. Yvette was still a regular at my office hours, but I had not known she would be singing in the contest. She wore an unzipped pleather jacket cinched at the waist with a thick red belt, and knee-high, purple pleather boots. Underneath her jacket she wore a knock-off Bathing Ape T-shirt, a brand that was fairly popular in Guiyang. This particular knockoff, however, had been done poorly. It had a picture of a purple gorilla underneath the words "Bathing Rape." Yvette sang a Madonna-esque version of "Don't Cry for Me, Argentina." Her voice was pure, she was poised, and her pronunciation—I was proud to note—was spot-on. I gave her a 90.

After Yvette finished, the judge I had spoken to earlier leaned over to look at my score card. "You are the professional judge, so I will just copy what you write," he told me. He went on to tell me of his position as vice chairman of the Youth Communist League and introduced himself as Carl. "I'm good at the politics, but the music I don't understand." He offered me a cigarette and, as the next act began, called someone on his cell phone. I appeared to be the only judge paying attention to the action on stage. This was typical of a Chinese audience: there were people on the phone, others were chatting with each other throughout the performances, still others sat reading newspapers. None of this was considered impolite.

I, on the other hand, was doing my best to listen to a slick young crooner's rendition of the Carpenters song "Yesterday Once More."

"Every sha-la-la-la, Every wo-wo-wo, Still shines," he sang, waving to the young women in the audience. As he hammed it up, I received a two-word text message on my phone:

Are you?

I did not recognize the number, nor did I understand this deeply existential question. Was Big Twin trying to get in touch with me? Her English was shaky, so the message could have been hers.

Who r u? I texted back.

The unnerving reply:

I am here to watch u. Can u see me?

Big Twin this was not. I had given my cell phone number to some of my students, and they had, in turn, given it to others in town, anyone hoping to practice English. I occasionally received messages from total strangers asking for friendship, advice, or some other kind of help. I replied:

Do you know what 'stalker' means?

A few minutes later I received an answer:

What is stalker? I m watching u. ☺

I decided not to respond, which was just as well because President Bill was excitedly calling me onto the stage. "It is time for a performance from the foreign teacher, Mike!" I had not been told that a performance was part of my duties as a judge, but I knew the audience would be polite no matter how poorly I performed.

I walked onto the stage to raucous applause. "Hello, Guiyang!" I yelled as the crowd roared. "Happiness every day!" I cried even louder. The audience reached a fever pitch.

I sang my go-to song, "I'm a Little Teapot," complete with the little teapot dance, and received Elvis-level adulation. As I was leaving the stage, I caught my first glimpse of Big Twin. She was waiting in the wings to perform. She was the next act.

I started feeling nervous.

Getting Big Twin into the contest was as simple as asking President Bill to put her on the list of finalists. He didn't even ask me who she was or why I wanted her to perform; he simply took her name, and that was that. All of the contestants were selected because of *guanxi* they had with judges or city leaders, so there was nothing particularly untoward about my lobbying efforts. Relationships were, as always, the only currency that really mattered in Guiyang. But Big Twin was the youngest performer, and while her singing was wonderful, her English skills were weak. Had I set her up to fail?

Big Twin stepped onto the stage to a smattering of applause. She was wearing acid-washed blue jeans, a sequined T-shirt, and had her long hair pulled back tightly in a ponytail. She was the only contestant who performed without makeup and without a personal cheering section. Her family was not in the audience. I was the only person in the room who knew who she was. Did this make her feel alone? Was she happy to be anonymous? How would the audience feel knowing this was a girl from a nearby village, of minority ethnicity, now working in a restaurant, hoping only to get some money for her sister's tuition?

Big Twin walked to the center of the stage and stood frozen as she waited for the music to begin. Her eyes were closed tightly as she began singing: *"Far across the ocean, I see you, I feel you."* I had flashbacks of Leonardo DiCaprio. I wished Big Twin would open her eyes. The crowd had fallen silent, and some were singing along. Céline Dion was huge in China.

Big Twin soon reached the chorus. She sang slowly and more of the audience joined her. By the time she reached the second verse, a wall of voices had joined in. She opened her eyes, smiled, and visibly relaxed, finishing the song to loud applause. She waved to me as she exited the stage, and received the highest overall score to that point in the contest, a 92 average from me and the other judges. Happily, the score held: Big Twin was a full point and a half better than her closest competitor, a lounge singer named Festival who performed "Unchained Melody."

I was beside myself. Here, in less than two hours, Big Twin had earned enough money to pay for nearly a semester of her sister's college education. Li Mei was wrong: my quick fix and overinvolvement *would* make a difference.

President Bill took the stage to announce the winner. "I am happy to announce that the judges have calculated the scores, and we are ready to give the prizes." Each contestant was in a line behind President Bill. Big Twin was holding hands with Yvette and Lemonade. She was beaming.

"The winner," said President Bill, "is Festival, for his performance of the 'Unchained Melody.'"

The crowd cheered madly. Big Twin continued to hold hands and smile. Carl, the judge to my left, was still on the phone. President Bill was shaking Festival's hand.

I tapped Carl on the shoulder. "This is wrong," I said, interrupting his conversation. "Festival did not have the top score." I pointed to the sheet we had used to tabulate the totals. "He finished second." Carl shrugged. The other two judges were equally disinterested.

Festival was given a bouquet of flowers, the cash prize, and received a standing ovation. He was led off the stage, weeping with joy.

I later learned why my scorecard did not match reality: Festival was President Bill's nephew. His *guanxi* assured his victory.

二十五

Democracy with Chinese Characteristics

The singing contest was another rough lesson in life with Chinese Characteristics. Big Twin had gotten into the contest due to *guanxi* and lost due to *guanxi*. Perhaps this was somehow fair, or at least cosmically just. But why hold a contest if the winner is foreordained? Was I the only one who hadn't understood the rules of the game? I thought about the WWF wrestling I had watched every weekend as a kid. I knew the bouts were fixed. I knew Hulk Hogan would never lose to the Iron Sheik. I had still loved every minute of the matches, and they still moved me to cheer and feel both nervous and exhilarated. If everyone else accepted that the singing contest was more WWF than genuine competition, what was the harm?

Li Mei was right: getting overinvolved was futile. Did that make Greg the Australian right as well? What about Coach Qin and Li Yuchun's river? I couldn't tell if the Guiyang way made sense and I was just out of my element, or if my fresh eyes were the only ones that could see the gangrenous corruption of the Guizhou system.

◇

On the final morning of class with Kevin and the undergraduates, I clawed my way out of a deep sleep with the nagging feeling I was not where I was supposed to be. I hauled my eyes open
and looked around my room. Everything was where I had left it
the night before, where it had been for the past two years. My
bed was pressed against the southern wall of the room. Above it
hung a grey tapestry featuring a sun setting over a rice farm. To
my left was a small window that looked out on a courtyard full
of stunted trees and unwanted cinderblocks. Above me hung a
mosquito net that protected me from being bitten as I slept. The
only other accoutrements in the room were a bureau full of
clothing and a knee-high dresser on top of which sat my clock,
a thick copy of *The Lord of the Rings*, and my Chinese-English
dictionary, both of which had gathered dust from months of
neglect. It was all so familiar, but something definitely felt out
of place. I breathed in the warm spring air, perfumed as always
with the faint scent of mold, and wracked my brain. I glanced at
the clock: 8:15 a.m.

I was late for class.

I bounded out of bed. Where was my opera-singing alarm
clock? This was the first day since my arrival that my neighbor
had not provided a wake-up serenade, Sichuan style. Why now?
Why my last full day of class?

The silence of the morning was the cause of my feeling of
unease—I had expected the singing, assuming it would wake
me (and greet the dawn) as it always had. Without it, I was late.
I felt out of sorts and out of place. To feel *out* of place, I realized,
meant you had to be *in* place to begin with. Anticipating my
neighbor's inconsiderate behavior, missing it . . . these struck
me as signs of successful acclimatization. I had made this little
apartment and all of its flaws my home. I no longer felt that the
patterns of this life were wholly foreign or that I was wearing
someone else's shoes and following someone else's calendar. It
was all mine. Perhaps home is simply a place where the things

that you ought to hate no longer drive you crazy. I smiled and looked at my emaciated body in the mirror. I was as Guizhou as I was ever going to get.

I threw on some shorts and a T-shirt, grabbed my book bag, and ran out the door. I ran past the stray dogs. I ran past the chickens pecking away at pebbles. I ran past the *you tiao* and banana salesman, the apartment compound up the hill from my own, the bathhouse, the basketball courts, up and up towards the Foreign Language Building. I arrived at my classroom at 8:30, half an hour late and completely winded.

I had prepared a lesson on the difference between the "sh" and "s" sounds. It wasn't much of a finale, but it was something that had long given the students trouble. Dandy, for example, often told me that my office was "his favorite place to shit." I had also asked Jennifer to deliver us a cake at exactly 10:00 a.m. It would be a nice surprise to celebrate the end of the term and the end of our time together.

On an ordinary day, the class would already be full of sleepy-eyed students. If the previous two years held true, Kitten would be cutting her hairs one by one with a nail clipper, Anvil would be drooling on her desk, fast asleep, and Yvette would be listening to BBC recordings on her MP3 player. I was ready to warm everyone up with a rousing rendition of "She Sells Seashells by the Seashore." Instead, I stared at empty desks, huffing and puffing alone.

Where was everyone? Had the students abandoned ship, thinking I wouldn't show up? I scanned the room searching for a clue. I looked at the grey floors and green walls. I looked at the faded picture of Marx hanging over the door. My gaze passed over the windows running along the south wall, all without glass. Wind whipped up chalk dust, filling the air with a slight haze. Fluttering in the haze was a note taped to the rickety wooden lectern at the front of the room. Perhaps this was the clue I was looking for. I glanced at the note: "No class today, Mike. Special Occasion." The handwriting was Kevin Chen's.

I stood breathing in the chalk dust for a few minutes. "Special Occasion." A Communist Party meeting, perhaps? Schedules at Gui Da, like schedules for the basketball team, were often invented on the fly. Anything written on paper or printed in a book was no more than an approximation of how a day might proceed rather than a fixed source of time management. If a student or teacher had an event scheduled with someone higher on the pecking order, and that person had a last-minute request, the rest of the day was reordered accordingly. I was low on the pecking order, so interruptions and changes were as much a part of my daily teaching experience as grammar and vocabulary.

I had long been used to trimming lessons designed for an hour down to twenty minutes, or reorganizing on the spot as students came and went. Kevin would always provide reasons for his classmates' absences or the changes in our schedule, announcing them at the beginning of class. He would stand and turn to his classmates. "Today, we must end class twenty minutes early so we can complete our military training." Or, "Today, Machine and Stone Crusher are absent because they have diarrhea." Military drills and diarrhea had caused minor disruptions. I had even lost entire classes to important party meetings. Missing the last class of the term, however, was just too much. I had lost the chance to tell my students good-bye.

I stood by the window with the note in hand. The minutes ticked away in silence. Eventually a loudspeaker crackled to life in the distance. Life at Gui Da had been full of loudspeaker announcements, from the 6:00 a.m. calisthenics routine that blared each morning near the basketball courts ("Touch your toes! One, two, three, four, TWO, two, three, four") to the Friday afternoon English lessons broadcast across campus. Isabel was the host of the radio show that broadcast the lessons. They ran from 3:00 to 3:30 p.m. every week and were pumped through the two dozen speakers spread around campus. When they spoke, there was no escaping their message. She could be heard from the main gate to the Foreign Language Building, and from the library to the Confucian Studies Center. I would hear her voice as I walked home from class at the end of each week. I looked forward to hearing it one last time later that day.

Isabel always chose something topical. "Today, we will learn the vocabulary for Valentine's Day!" she had chirped a few months before. "All Americans celebrate this day as the birth-day of Romance." Isabel had asked me to help her write a dia-logue about the meaning of True Love. "Tell Guizhou about your Jack and Rose story," she said to me with a smirk. I told everyone about my first girlfriend, a nice Jewish girl I met in Israel. Our relationship ended when she rooted against the Chi-cago Bulls, my favorite basketball team at the time. I knew I could never love an Orlando Magic fan.

Today's topic, the final of the term, was "saying good-bye." Isabel had run her farewell speech by me to make sure it was perfect. "This is the last time I'll ever be on the radio," she told me during my office hour. "I hope it is flawless." Isabel planned to advise her classmates to make sure they said good-bye care-fully and from the heart. "Since the future cannot be known and everything is changeable, I beg all of you to find the people you have come to love and express yourself with fervency. You will never have this chance again."

Isabel's voice would soon fill the Gui Da campus. For now, it was a different voice echoing from the loudspeakers. I looked out of the classroom towards the source of the static-filled sound. "*Women de xuesheng dou yao huilai*," said the voice. *All students must report immediately.*

I noticed a long line in front of the school auditorium, a squat stone building a few hundred yards away. A number of my students were in the line, standing beneath the Chinese flag. Beyond the flag was a bright red banner with Chinese charac-ters stenciled in black: 贵州大学 共产党 投票站. I recog-nized the last three characters: 投票, meaning "vote," and 站,

meaning "station." If my Peace Corps training wasn't failing me, I was looking at a polling center. Dozens of my students were apparently about to cast votes.

I leaned out the window hoping to get a better look at the banner. China and democracy? Perhaps I was misreading the sign. Or perhaps I had gotten China and politics as wrong as I had gotten China and religion. Teacher Qing could read William James. Jennifer could fast on Yom Kippur. Democracy, too, could be imported and imbued with Chinese Characteristics. I wondered what they would be.

As I had these thoughts, a familiar, pudgy figure walked past my window at a brisk pace. It was Jackie, the Crazy English devotee. I yelled to him and he looked over with a start. He was flushed and a bit bug-eyed.

"Jackie, what does that sign say?"

"Oh!" he replied, eyes nervously darting from side to side and then back to me. He turned to the banner. "The sign says 'Guizhou University Communist Party Election Place.' We are selecting people to send to the People's Congress in Beijing." I had read something about this in the *China Daily*, a thin, airy English-language newspaper that carried state-sanctioned stories from around the world. The paper was light on journalism but did offer summaries of major events in Chinese politics.

My eyes widened. "Wow! That's great! But no one told me class was cancelled."

"Yes," Jackie said, his nervousness seeming to increase. "The voting is required of all students, so no one can attend class this morning." Jackie got a dark look on his face. "Kevin should have told you."

"Yeah, he wrote me a note," I replied, waving it at him. Casting a vote was obviously more important than learning how to enunciate the difference between "shuck" and "suck." It was even more important than our final class. I tried not to feel self-pity. "Who is on the ballot?" I asked.

"I'm not sure," he said, slowly backing away from the window. "But you can vote for anyone you want."

"Vote for me," I said with a wink. Jackie shook his head slowly, his body frozen stiffly in place. We stared at each other in silence until he snapped out of his torpor, turned, and ran away.

I decided to head towards the auditorium and the polling place to try to find the rest of Kevin's class. If I found them, I could thank them for our two years and tell them good-bye, one by one. It was not an ideal way to say farewell, but it was better than nothing.

I walked through the empty Foreign Language Building, hearing my footsteps echoing in the cool hallway. The only other sound I heard was whispering coming from a classroom at the end of the hall. I peeked inside and found two students hiding under a desk. They were sharing a bag of soy milk, squatting next to each other and holding hands. I entered the room and saw who they were. "Shitty, Kitten, what are you doing under the desk?" The girls were shocked to hear my voice and jumped up.

"Shhh," they implored me in unison. Shitty looked at me mischievously. "Mike, be quiet. We are hiding because we do not want to vote. But if they catch us avoiding it, we will be punished!"

"Why don't you want to vote?" I asked.

Kitten shook her head. "It is better to hide and avoid the problem."

"I don't understand," I told her. "What is the 'problem'?"

"We don't know anything important!" Shitty interjected, before Kitten could respond. "The leaders should do what is best. What does voting have to do with it?"

I mumbled something about accountability, the will of the people, and I might have quoted Lincoln. It wasn't impressive. In fact, my plea was downright desperate. Perhaps I was feeling pressure to end my time in China with an exclamation mark of do-gooding and volunteer success. Perhaps I wanted to redeem myself for failing to help Big Twin. Whatever the reason, I felt like I could influence Shitty and Kitten for the better. As Guizhou as I had become, I was still stubbornly American.

Kitten, however, was on her game and ready to put me in place: "I recently read that the FBI has been spying on Americans." The warrantless wiretapping of American citizens—big news in the U.S. in 2007—had been *huge* news for weeks in China, pumped into the information cycle by the media barons in the propaganda wing of the Communist Party. If the American government was spying on its own people under the banner of National Security, why couldn't other governments? *China Daily* and the rest of the media were running wild with this argument, seemingly giddy to have received a gift-wrapped rationale for intrusive behavior. "Happy Birthday, Tyranny," said the card attached to the gift. "Hope you enjoy the political cover this will give your regime. Yours Truly, Dick Cheney."

Kitten seemed to have read the gift card. "Americans have democracy and still lose their freedoms," she told me. She didn't want to waste her time voting.

I sensed an opportunity, a final moment to shine as a Peace Corps volunteer. I listened to the girls, waiting for my chance to make a difference.

Shitty offered her thoughts. "Americans get upset at our Communist Party when it freezes the Internet to protect us from immoral things," she said, with consternation on her face, "but they don't get very upset when the FBI does something similar. This is a double standard."

"Maybe," I said. I didn't agree with what the girls were saying, but I did feel good that they were saying it. This was a conversation that simply could not have happened when I first arrived, or even a year into my time at Gui Da. It had taken two full years for many of my students and friends to become comfortable enough with me to really tell me what they felt. And so while I couldn't instantly save anyone from poverty, I could at least have a few conversations that introduced a new perspective. It wasn't much, but it wasn't nothing.

"You know," I continued, "a lot of Americans don't support the government when it does these things. They think the FBI and the president broke the law."

Shitty was having none of it: "The law in America is meaningless if the government does not have to follow it."

I nodded. "That's true, but if our leaders break the law, we can choose someone new. This is why voting is important: to hold the government accountable."

"But . . ." Kitten said, collecting her thoughts as she sipped soy milk. "George Bush cannot be elected again anyway. So there is nothing to hold him to the law."

"And maybe he knows best, anyway," Shitty added. "After all, he is powerful."

Kitten jumped in again: "Democracy is too chaotic. We should just listen to the leaders."

I took a deep breath. Discussing politics, government, or civics had always been a dicey proposition in Guiyang. The conversations were obstacle courses of vocabulary, terminology, and assumption. Every explanation required a definition; every definition required a history lesson; every history lesson required an interpretation. Why didn't the FBI follow the law? What was the law? What did the Patriot Act actually say? Was it constitutional? There wasn't time to give Shitty a lesson on the separation of powers, or tell Kitten about *Cherokee Nation v. Georgia*.

"You guys are killing me," I told the girls.

Kitten tilted her head and made a "v" with her eyebrows.

"Never mind," I told her, waving off her unasked question about the meaning of this colloquialism. "It's slang, and it's not very important." I reached under the table and grabbed the girls. "But what *is* important is voting. We can't always trust our leaders, but we can choose them carefully. You have a chance to do so right now."

The girls stood before me and reached out once again to hold hands. They each stood no more than five foot two, and together they probably outweighed me by only a few pounds. Kitten's bleaching had faded over the course of the term and she now looked more human. Shitty had a new haircut that left blond bangs dangling over her eyes. "You just cannot understand," she told me. The girls shot back under the desk. "We will stay here," Kitten said with finality.

I sighed. "Well, I'm going to the polling place." Shitty shrugged. Kitten grinned. I left them beneath their table.

◇

As I exited the building, I ran headlong into Kevin. He had been coming regularly to my postmodern lit class ever since our Walmart heart-to-heart. He had even participated on occasion. The graduate students found him adorable and cooed whenever he made a good point. He loved every minute of it. Kevin was a serious student and I knew he would be disappointed to miss our final lesson together. At the same time, I hoped he would take the voting more seriously than Shitty and Kitten.

"Sorry, Mike," he said as we collided. "Did you receive my note?"

"I did," I said. "It's a shame to miss our last class."

"It is horrible to miss class," he said. "But today is an important day." Kevin was distracted and looking past me into the Foreign Language Building. "Mike," he continued, "there is a big problem. Have you seen Pussy and Shitty? I have to catch them because they are not ready to vote."

"She's not Pussy anymore, she's Kitten," I reminded him. I paused before saying more; I wondered if I should misdirect him, dodge the question, or tell him the truth. How much trouble would the girls be in for hiding?

I decided to snitch: "They're inside, hiding under a desk."

Kevin's face hardened and I immediately regretted my decision. "They should know better," he told me.

"Will you punish them?" I asked.

Kevin sighed. "I'm supposed to. I should require them to pay a fine."

"Is the voting really that important?"

I received a stony stare. "Does voting really matter in your America? Isn't the power really in the hands of the rich and the corporations?"

I was taken aback by the vitriol in his response. "Well, that's a little cynical," I responded.

He shrugged. "You have your form of democracy, which we call Corporate Democracy, and we have our form which we call Democracy with Chinese Characteristics." He said this off-handedly, perhaps quoting from a newspaper or textbook. He then looked around to make sure we were alone. Fifteen minutes earlier, Jackie had taken the same look around, but their body language was not at all the same. Jackie had been twitchy and closed, stepping farther away from me with each sentence of our short conversation. Kevin seemed confident and put his hand on my arm. He looked right and left with a hint of conspiracy in his eyes. "Actually, I don't really care. To tell you the truth, this is all bullshit."

My eyes widened. Shitty and Kitten were simply hiding from the voting process. Kevin was bold enough to insult it head-on. "What, exactly, is bullshit?" I asked him.

Kevin pulled his hand from my arm and ran it over his cross-cropped hair. "Everything is bullshit." We stood together for a moment. "Mike, can you give me some advice?" Kevin was looking at me earnestly. "Can you tell me if you think I should punish the two girls?"

I crossed my arms. "No, Kevin, I don't."

Kevin seemed immensely relieved to hear this and nodded.

"I agree," he said, taking a deep breath. "But it is my job. I am supposed to force them to participate. Americans understand democracy already, but we are still learning." Kevin paused again. "Are Americans required to vote?"

"Nope. And most Americans don't bother."

Kevin nodded again. "Democracy is bullshit."

I quickly started shaking my head, realizing I had given Kevin the wrong impression with my flippant comment about American apathy. Before I could rebuild his faith in voting, he thanked me, shook my hand, and entered the Foreign Language Building. As he stepped into the building, the clouds above parted and a beam of light shined down on me, highlighting for a brief moment the worst Peace Corps volunteer on earth.

◇

I began the short walk to the center of campus towards the polling station. I had to redeem myself. I couldn't let my interaction with Kevin be the cherry on top of the shit pie I was cooking up as a Peace Corps legacy. I would spend a few moments engaged in the promotion of the Bush Doctrine: I would be a democracy lover, a smiling beacon of the people, by the people, and for the people.

I felt like I might not have to work very hard. There was an energy in the air and a growing crowd. Perhaps the cynicism expressed by Shitty, Kitten, and Kevin was a minority opinion. I wove my way between groups of students who were chatting and goofing around. Each class monitor was trying to arrange his classmates into a line, but none were having much luck. There were too many distractions. Women in Bouyei headdresses were selling baked sweet potatoes out of burn barrels for ten cents a pop, and men in cheap suits with Zhongnanhai brand cigarettes dangling from their lips were hocking pirated DVDs. "American DVDs for sale," one of them told me. "Want to buy some?"

I shook my head. "Not right now," I said, "because there's one thing Americans love more than cheap DVDs, and that's democracy!" I slapped the man on the back. He looked at me nervously with his eyebrows raised. I moved on, feeling like a schmuck.

The scene around me was half Election Day, half county fair. I was soon surrounded by spectators. Most students at Gui Da had gotten over the shock of seeing a white man wandering around, but some still found me fascinating. This might have been particularly true at an election. I had long been seen by the Gui Da community as a great source for information on romance and religion. Perhaps now I could be a source for information on democracy as well.

"Who are you going to vote for?" I asked a group of girls who were staring at me and whispering to each other. Most of them blushed and averted their eyes, but the tallest looked me up and down. "It doesn't matter," she told me. "We vote; the teachers choose. This is just for fun."

"Huh?" I grunted. "I don't understand . . ."

She rolled her eyes, causing her friends to collectively turn an even deeper shade of red. "We are told who to vote for. If we don't listen, our votes are thrown out. The winner has already been chosen."

"Oh," I grunted. Perhaps singing contests and national elections were both carried out in the WWF tradition. "In that case, why do you bother voting?"

"We have to," said the tall girl as she and the gaggle moved away from me with a surge in the crowd. She yelled a final line before disappearing: "Our class monitors demand it!"

Poor Kevin. His task for the day was to force his disinterested (or perhaps surly) classmates to waste time "voting" in a fixed election for a person who would have no power. I, too, would feel upset in his position. It *was* bullshit.

A Guiyang election, I realized, was not the place to make my last stand as a Peace Corps volunteer. It did, however, turn out to be a good place to say my good-byes. I soon found Kevin's class in a single-file line along the side of the auditorium. They seemed as relieved to see me as I was to see them. "We thought we might never see you," Yvette gushed, breaking out of line to give me a hug. "How did you find us?"

"I just followed the noise," I replied. Other students peeled away from the building to come and hug me or shake my hand. Somehow, one of them produced a cake, handing it to me in a long, pink box.

"Ms. He gave this to us," Gordon explained. His English, after two years of hard work, was now clear and confident. "She said she wanted to surprise you with it." Gordon took the cake out of my hands, put it on the ground, and squatted down to cut it into pieces. He distributed them one by one to his happy classmates. "You are so kind, Mike," he said as he did his work. His voice was shaking as he spoke, and his lip twitched. "No teacher has ever been so kind to us." Gordon took a piece of cake in his hand and held it out to me. When I took it, he burst into tears. "We will never forget you!" he wailed. Other students started crying as well.

"Hey everyone," I said softly, "let's try and be happy. Let's think about all the fun we had and all we learned about each other." I took a deep breath, fighting back tears myself. We ate quietly until a whistle blew. It was time for my class to head into the auditorium and vote. They filed into the polling booths in silence.

Yvette was the final student in line. "We cherish what we have learned from you," she said, pausing with a foot on the threshold of the building. She thought for a moment then stepped towards me and gave me another hug. "I want to say good-bye to you with a famous Chinese sentence." Yvette released me but kept a grip on both of my hands. "It is *renshi zhi neng lai zi youyi*. It means 'understanding can only be built upon friendship.' I know you are a friendship volunteer, and for my classmates I want to say: I hope you can go back to America and help them understand us a little more." She released me, turned, and headed into the polling place. She would cast her vote in a fixed election. Yvette knew the vote didn't count. She also knew it didn't have to count to matter.

二十六

Jia You

The text message glowing on my phone was simple and to the point:

8pm, my home

Coach Qin was calling a rare weekend meeting. I packed my backpack with high-tops, sneakers, both my home and away jerseys, a T-shirt, shorts, and khakis. Did we have a late-night game? Was this a team dinner, or would we down a few cases of beer? Would we, for some reason, meet with school or city officials? Would we end up lifting rusty barbells and running laps? There was no way to know for sure. I needed to be ready for anything.

Coach lived on the other side of campus, not far from Jennifer and Vivian. His apartment was equipped with some rare amenities: he had a small washing machine and a fully Western bathroom. Whenever I visited his house, I prayed for the movement of my bowels. I felt joy whenever I settled onto his toilet, a feeling I imagined was only matched by a bear heading to his cave to hibernate for the winter or a whale getting pushed back into the ocean after beaching on a sand dune.

I was massaging my belly as I walked, in the hope of getting things moving, when Ah Ge pulled up beside me. He was walking with his usual swagger and wearing a larger than usual grin. He raised his hand in a salute and said "Hello!" in English.

"Did you hear the news?" he asked, continuing to practice his English. He had improved quite a bit over the last six months, always happy to hear my suggestions on pronunciation. "We have been promoted to the number one game." He waved a single finger in the air. "We can prove we are the great ones!" Ah Ge was always bubbly, but tonight he was downright giddy. He threw his arm around my shoulder and walked with me the rest of the way to Coach Qin's.

The team was already assembled in the living room when we arrived. Everyone was buzzing with excitement. Coach greeted Ah Ge with a thumbs-up, and me with a high five. He gestured for us to sit on a pair of plastic stools he had set out for us. He quieted the team.

"Each of you has worked hard this year," he began, as everyone fell silent. "You have not always succeeded, and each of you can still improve. Nevertheless, there is much to be proud of." Coach paused here, either for dramatic effect or because he wanted to choose his next words carefully. "The city leaders have decided to reward us by letting us play in the final game of the season." Ah Ge gave a yell of excitement. His legs were bouncing up and down as he sat on his stool, and he was twitching with enthusiasm. Coach raised a hand, palm forward, to settle his captain and proceeded with his speech. "If we win, we will certainly bring a lot of happiness and praise to our school and to our team. If we lose, it will be no major problem, but it will mean we did not work hard enough. I hope we can win." There had been no play-offs, no objective methodology for determining who would play the final game, and no advance warning that the season was ending. I didn't care; from what I had seen we were the best team in the city and deserved to play in whatever version of a championship Guiyang would offer. "The game is tomorrow afternoon," Coach concluded. "Be ready to leave on the team bus at 2:00 p.m."

Ah Ge leaped up from his stool and pumped his arm in the air. "*Jia you*," he yelled. The phrase literally meant "add oil," but its figurative meaning fell somewhere between "Let's go!" "Booyakasha," and "Who's your daddy?" The team leaped up and joined Ah Ge in a chant.

"*Jia you, jia you, jia you!*" I joined in as well, hopping from my stool and locking arms with Ah Ge. We leaped up and down in place. The others crowded around, moshing together in the center of the living room. Da Bao slapped me on the back. Chen Chen did a little Michael Jackson dance, complete with a crotch grab and a moonwalk. Other players were furiously sending text messages. I soon did the same, shooting messages to Big Twin, Jennifer, and whoever else I could think of. I wanted everyone to see the game, to have their final impression of me be one in which I was effective and competent. The basketball court was as good a place as any for me to leave this impression.

But what kind of game would it be? Would we still play by the friendship-first rule? Were Communists still allowed to foul others without penalty? Would I have to play nice? Or would this be a no-holds-barred, honest match of skills? If so, I was sure we would win. There had been some tough games during the season, and we had even lost a few, but I had never played much more than a half. Coach always balanced winning with political sensitivity. The currents of the politics he was playing were imperceptible to me, but I always followed his instructions closely. There were players I wouldn't guard, shots I wouldn't take, and portions of games where I would simply head to the opposite team's bench and build *guanxi*. At times I felt as much a mascot as a player. Nevertheless, every game I had played was fun, and I was sure the final game would be no different. Perhaps Coach could even use me to my full effectiveness. I wouldn't mind playing at least one game at full speed and with all my effort.

The more I thought about the game, the more excited I became. What a great way to end a two-year experience! I was ready to go out a winner.

There was, however, a catch. Coach sent a few of the youngest players out to buy beers for the team, handing them money. He then pulled me aside. "This is a great honor for the team," he told me. "But the city leaders have decided we will play against the military school." I groaned. The Taiwan Problem again? "I don't know if you'll be able to play," Coach said, shaking his head.

I took a deep breath and felt blood rising to my face. Coach massaged my shoulders. "*Meibanfa*," he told me. "We just have to wait and see. The game is not at the military school, so they might let you play. It's not up to us."

Ah Ge had been eavesdropping on the conversation. To my surprise he started yelling rapid-fire curses. Coach tried to slow him down, but Ah Ge was turning red and began pacing one of the hallways. I couldn't understand everything he was saying, but I knew he was outraged that I might be banned. His histrionics caught the attention of the rest of the team. Coach put both hands in front of him in a calming gesture and explained the situation to them. They split down the middle, half simply shrugging and telling the others not to worry, the other half joining Ah Ge in frustration and anger.

The beers soon arrived, and Coach Qin poured everyone a small glass. "Just one toast tonight, because I want you all to rest," he said. "We can celebrate properly tomorrow after the game." Ah Ge had a sour look on his face. He had not picked up his glass, and Coach eyed him, waiting. Eventually, the cloud over Ah Ge's head broke and he picked up his glass with a sigh. He offered the toast.

"I have been happy to be the team captain this year," he told everyone. "Whatever happens tomorrow, and whoever plays, we can be proud of ourselves. *Gan bei*." We downed our shots.

◇

The next afternoon, I laced up my sneakers, put on my red double-zero jersey, and headed for the front gate of Gui Da to board the team bus. I checked my phone. Big Twin had texted to let me know she could get out of her cooking job for the day and would make the game. Jennifer also promised she would be there. Kevin was in. Isabel sent word she would do her best to attend and that she might bring Qing Fong as well. I would see both women in class the following Tuesday, and Isabel's message reminded me I needed to start planning this final lesson. I wanted our last two hours together—the last I would ever teach as a Peace Corps volunteer—to go off without a hitch. I promised myself I would get to work as soon as the game was over.

The team was silent as we rode north on Huaxi highway, each player engaged in his own version of meditation. Some listened to MP3 players, others had their eyes closed. Some just stared out the window. I didn't know what to do. I didn't even know if I would be playing in the game. Coach had given me no indication of my status. I would either be his starting power forward or the loudest cheerleader on his bench. Either way, I would be positive and support the team. There was no reason to pout this late in my time in Guizhou. The system was what it was and nothing would change it.

The ride from campus to the gym would take about an hour. At the halfway point, not far from the Wang village, Ah Ge jumped up and ran to the front of the bus. He was half smiling, half grimacing. "Stop the bus!" he yelled to the driver.

"I can't stop now, you'll be late for the game." The driver waved Ah Ge back to his seat.

"*Aiyo!*" Ah Ge yelled. "I have to take a shit." He was holding his backside and looking panicky. I recognized the look; he was doing the diarrhea dance. Ah Ge was not going to make it for thirty more minutes. My estimate, based on the fear in his eyes and the veins bulging out of his neck, was that he had no more than five minutes to liftoff. "When I get nervous I have to shit!" he yelled. The meditations of the team were interrupted and everyone stared at Ah Ge. I laughed out loud. Coach shook his head. The rest of the team started howling and mocking him. The bus driver looked back at Coach, taking his eyes completely off the road for the duration of a short conversation. Coach told him to drive on. Ah Ge put his head on the dashboard and moaned. Da Bao joined him at the front of the bus, handing him a plastic bag.

"Just use this," he said before running back to his seat.

Ah Ge held the bag with one hand, his butt with the other, and groaned through gritted teeth. He hid himself by walking down the stairs at the front of the bus that led to the door. I could still see him from the neck up as he squatted behind the low wall that led down to the door, but at least he had a bit of privacy. Was he really going to crap in a bag? He was fumbling around. His eyes began to tear. He gave one more loud cry. And then—visibly—he released.

The sounds of Ah Ge's pregame indigestion hit the team moments before the smells. Coach was still shaking his head. I was laughing so hard I, like Ah Ge, had tears in my eyes. Those in the front of the bus were gagging.

"Paper!" Ah Ge cried after he had finished. "Give me paper!" He half stood, rising above the wall to chest level.

Da Bao returned to the front of the bus and handed Ah Ge a newspaper. Ah Ge grabbed it and shoved Da Bao away. He squatted back down. I didn't know exactly how he was cleaning himself, but after a few moments, he leaned over and pushed the lever to open the door of the bus. We were driving at about thirty miles per hour on the highway. Ah Ge tossed the plastic bag out the door. It flew in a high arc towards the sidewalk, tracing the path of a plump goose shot in midflight by a hunter, and landed with a hideous splat, scattering its wet contents against the side of a building.

Ah Ge closed the door as we raced on. He looked at the team, grinned, and took a bow. We applauded and he returned to his seat. I heard him sigh with relief. The tension had been broken, and the team began its usual chatter.

I was glad the bag hadn't hit anyone. I was also glad I didn't get nervous in the same way as Ah Ge. I had come a long way in my squatting since my airport disaster two years before, but I doubted I had the dexterity to crap in a bag. Some things would always be beyond my abilities.

二十七

The Big Game

We pulled into the parking lot in front of the city's largest gymnasium and headed inside in a single-file line. The team was feeling loose, but I could sense more tension than usual. I kept looking over at Coach Qin, waiting for a clue about my fate. Still nothing. We walked up a flight of stairs and paused at the doorway that led onto the court. "Do your best today," Coach said, walking from player to player and shaking hands with each of us. When he reached me, he held my hand firmly and looked directly into my eyes. I waited for the verdict. He moved on without a word.

Once reaching the front of the line, Coach threw open the doors and Ah Ge ran out into the gym leading the team in a few laps around the court. The other team was already warming up. I was last in line and jogged with my head down following the feet of the player in front of me. We did three laps. We did our layups. We sprinted. We stretched. Still nothing from Coach.

After warming up I sat on our team's bench and looked out into the stands. There were perhaps a hundred people in attendance. I saw Jennifer and Vivian. I saw Kevin sitting with Shitty. They were holding hands. The sight of the two of them giggling and flirting broke any remaining tension that had been building in my chest. I caught Kevin's eye and gave him a thumbs-up. I could see him blushing from fifty yards away.

Big Twin was also in the crowd. She waved to me and gave me a *jia you!* at the top of her lungs. I was glad to give her an excuse to take a one-day vacation and waved her over. She ran towards me. Big Twin looked older now, many years older than when I had first met her. Her hands were rough, and the skin on her face less smooth. She had also lost her rail-thin prepubescence and put a bit of padding on her hips and cheeks. Her eyes, however, were still those of a little girl. She grabbed hold of my forearm and thanked me for inviting her.

"Who is your friend?" Chen Chen asked as I chatted with Little Twin. He was sitting on the bench next to me, retying his high-tops.

"This is Big Twin, a friend of mine who lives nearby. She came to support us." Big Twin moved so that she was half hidden behind me. She shyly pulled me in a bit closer. Chen Chen moved his head so he could get a better look at her. I was waiting for some sort of insensitive comment about her Bouyei appearance, or her shabby clothing. Instead, Chen Chen told Big Twin he recognized her from the Guiyang City Spring Festival English Singing Contest.

"You were the best singer," he told her. "You should have won." Chen Chen finished tying his shoe and ran back onto the court.

Big Twin's eyes were huge and her mouth was agape. She didn't say a word. "You're famous!" I told her. Still no response. "Do you think he's handsome?" I teased.

Big Twin was nonplussed. "He's a little bit ugly," she said. I nodded and we chatted for another few minutes before I sent Big Twin back to her seat. I started my final bit of stretching and scanned the court. The military college had finished warming up, and both teams were huddling for some last-minute instructions from their coaches. I hopped up off the bench and leaned into our team circle. Coach was squatting in the middle over a small white board. He was diagramming our defensive scheme and reminding everyone of their assignments. I peeked outside of the huddle and looked for Ichabod Crane, the referee who had banned me from the first game against the military school. I was relieved to note that he was not one of the two officials standing at center court waiting for tip-off. One of them blew his whistle. The game was about to begin.

I took the court as I normally would. I looked out of the corners of my eyes at the officials, at Coach, at the other team's bench, at the crowd. I tried to make myself as innocuous as possible. Each step I took towards center court made me more certain I would be ejected from the game. Shui lined up in the center circle for the tip-off. I stood nearby, feet set wide apart. This was as far as I had gotten against the military team in our last meeting. I held my breath.

One official went to the center of the court, ball in hand. The other looked at each player. When his eyes rested on me, he put his whistle in his mouth. When he blew it, I felt a guillotine of Chinese frustration drop. I lowered my head helplessly.

But I was the only one who wasn't suddenly moving. The whistle hadn't been for me; it had been blown to start the game. My head shot up. The ball was already halfway down the court towards the opposing team's basket. I spirited into defensive position. An opposing player immediately blew a layup. I jumped and pulled in the rebound.

I held the ball and took a deep breath. The trip to the game had included a teammate crapping in a bag; my cheering section included a girl from a tiny village forced to go to work at age twelve; my team nickname was Friendship Jew. But the hoop was still ten feet high. A rebound was still a rebound. As long as I was allowed to play the game, the differences surrounding it faded away.

◇

Unfortunately, the game itself was somewhat anticlimactic. The military team was not terrible, but it was far from the best we had played that season. I was careful not to foul anyone, or even box anyone out with much gusto. I avoided contact. Still, the military players missed open shots and played lackadaisical defense. It was more of a pickup game than a championship game, and I played even less than my usual half. Coach gave me an apologetic look when he took me out about five minutes into the second quarter. He knew I wanted more minutes. Nevertheless, I was happy to head to the opposing bench for my meet and greet. I was curious to see if the opposing players would mention the first game we had played. I decided to ask about it.

"That had nothing to do with us," said the military team's center. He wore the same jersey number I had on, and he was drenched in sweat. He was, by far, their best player, and had scored nearly twenty points. He played seriously, but like everyone else he treated his opponents with respect. He made sure to help people up who had fallen, and he didn't take advantage when our coach put in some of our smaller, weaker players. The game wasn't quite over, but he had already untied his shoes and taken off his jersey. "That was that strange referee. He's crazy! But what can we do about it?"

"So there's no real rule about foreigners playing against your team?"

"Of course not," he laughed. "That would be ridiculous. But he's the official, so he makes the rules."

It was as good a summary of life in Guiyang as I could think of.

I posed for a few pictures and returned to our bench. We won the game by a dozen points and got a certificate in a brief ceremony. Ah Ge was also honored as the best point guard in the city. He had played only a few minutes in this game, running off at least twice more to use the bathroom. Still, he was smiling and bouncing with pride.

After the ceremony, Chen Chen powered up his boom box and played a farewell song as we exited the building. It was not Queen's "We Are the Champions." It was not even the Black Eyed Peas' "My Humps." Instead, it was Li Yuchun's newest hit, "My Kungfu."

Ah Ge patted me on the butt after the ceremony as we walked back to the team bus. "I knew it would all work out," he said, head bobbing to the music. "Things always work out the way they are supposed to." He started singing along with Li Yuchun. "*Trust the universe,*" he belted, closing his eyes and putting his heart into his singing. "*The world will stop for you only if you trust it.*" The rest of the team joined in. I was enjoying the song, but I didn't know the lyrics. I could only listen.

二十八

A Final Class

I had one final class to prepare, my final meeting with the post-graduates. I planned meticulously. I had never had a more enjoy-able group of students. I knew each member of the class well. I could anticipate what would give them difficulty and what would inspire them. I felt comfortable challenging them, and they had grown comfortable with each other. Jennifer, Vivian, and Kevin had helped loosen up the class dynamic and spring term had been even better than the fall. I looked forward to our last meet-ing with a combination of happiness, nostalgia, and nervous energy. I wanted desperately for things to end well.

Our best discussions of the year had always focused on poetry, and this would be the topic of the final lesson. China has a rich poetic tradition, from the days of the first emperor right up through the days of the Communist Party. Chairman Mao him-self was fond of putting quill to parchment. He wrote in the clas-sical Tang-dynasty style and took great pride as a wordsmith. In the 1960s, those interested in earning Maoist brownie points would memorize the Chairman's poems. I read a few myself and was surprised by how tender and wistful they seemed. "Two

Birds: A Dialogue" and "The Fairy Cave Inscription" are not the titles you expect from a man responsible for 50 million deaths.

My students had a genuine affection for Mao's poetry. "Chinese language is made for poems," Isabel once told me.

"We believe Chinese is not ideal for the digital age," Qing Fong had added during my office hour, "but it is just right for artistic expression." Qing Fong had opened up slowly as the weeks had passed, but she was still mostly a mystery to me. I did, however, now know that she liked Mao's politics as much as she liked his poetry. She was as ideological as any student I had ever met in China.

The others in the class enjoyed postmodern poetry far more than anything from Mao. For our final class, I chose two poems that were simple enough to understand but deep enough to analyze. I hoped the poems would serve as summaries of what we had learned, while leaving the students with further questions to ponder. I also hoped they would get under Qing Fong's skin and finally bring her fully into our discussions. This, more than anything, was my goal for the final lesson. I didn't want to go an entire year with one of my smartest students remaining silent in class. Step one had been our discussions during office hours. This was my last shot to draw her out in a way that could teach the other students.

◇

We spent the day working with Charles Bukowski's "My Father" and Allen Ginsberg's "America." The students learned that Bukowski's father was a Communist-hating Cold Warrior of the 1950s. His dad was so conservative that he called FDR "a goddamned Red." The poem includes Bukowski's reaction to his father's dogma: he decides that if his dad wants to be rich, then he wants to be a "bum." He chooses a life of sloth and poverty as a subversion of the American ideal of competition and wealth. In essence, Bukowski rejects the raving capitalism of his father by seeking a socialist paradise among the poor. But he learns that the bums—the socialists—are just as pathetic as his dad. He thus finds himself "caught between [his] father and the bums," drifting and lost. The poem ends with his father's death and a one-word summary of his life: "wasted."

Ginsberg is much more hopeful. He, too, rails against the hypocrisy and foolishness of right-wing Americans, sarcastically adopting the voice of an anti-Communist. "America, it's them bad Russians . . . and them Chinamen. And them Russians." But rather than leveling equal sarcasm at those on the left, Ginsberg defiantly states, "You should have seen me reading Marx." He is proud of his progressive politics: "America I used to be a communist when I was a kid and I'm not sorry."

For Bukowski, socialism, like any other "ism," is something only a fool or a demagogue follows. Bukowski mocks socialists mercilessly, calling them nothing more than bitter, failed capitalists. For Ginsberg, on the other hand, socialism is "angelic" and "sincere." It offers a way out of the horrors of the modern world.

As usual, the students came to class having read carefully and critically. I reviewed a bit of vocabulary and helped clarify a line or two of poetry. After about ten minutes of this basic preparation, we were ready for our final discussion. "Who would like to start?" I asked.

Qing Fong's hand shot in the air. She was flushed and looked downright pissed off. "How can Bukowski call Communists 'bums'?" she said in a confident voice. "Communism for China means independence and an end to imperialism." I gave myself a mental pat on the back. The conversation couldn't have started any better, and it was my wallflower who had started it.

Qing Fong concluded her thought: "What does Bukowski want instead?"

I looked around the room, hoping to stay in the background. After a short pause, Isabel, seated directly to Qing Fong's right, responded. "I think Bukowski is really rejecting his father more than he is rejecting Communism. So I can accept this."

Qing Fong scowled. I wondered if she was thinking something like, "That's easy for a rich girl from Shanghai to say . . . but what about life for a poor girl like me?" She said something in the same spirit though a bit less direct: "Communism once brought us equality. Who can reject that?"

I asked how many people in class were members of the Communist Party. No answer was forthcoming. Eventually, Isabel said, "Some of us are party members, some of us are not." I looked around the room, observing an awkward silence.

"Is this an embarrassing question?" I asked. "It seems like the room has grown colder."

Kevin raised his hand. I was glad I had invited him to join the postgraduates. He always added something to our discussions, and seemed far happier here than with Jackie and the other undergrads. "It is not shameful to be in the party. I am in it. But to be honest, it has no meaning one way or the other. I joined to help me get a job. It doesn't mean anything else." Heads nodded in agreement. Joining the party was a resumé builder, not a political statement. It had no ideological meaning.

I turned my attention to Qing Fong: "If Communism has no meaning in China today, then why do you defend it so vigorously? Who cares if Bukowski thinks Communists are bums?"

Qing Fong furled her brow. "It is because our Communism seems so beautiful. I'm no fool—I know that China is changing and developing rapidly. I know that Reform and Opening have ended the old ways, and that rather than socialism we have socialism with Chinese Characteristics. But how could anyone prefer the ideals of capitalism over the ideals of Communism? I just can't believe that."

"Well," I asked the class, "what does Bukowski think of capitalism, as represented by his father?"

Isabel raised a hand again. She was wearing her usual sundress, her long hair cascading over her shoulders. "Bukowski calls his father a waste." She ran her fingers through her hair as she spoke. "Therefore, perhaps he believes capitalism is a waste. I wish I could have this confidence in my ideas." Isabel had recently gotten word that Professor Fei had approved her graduate thesis. She would soon return to Shanghai and her husband. She was happy to be heading home, but worried about job prospects.

"Capitalism is not a waste," Isabel continued. "Capitalism has no values other than money, but that's all that makes sense in the world. We all want to be rich. So maybe we are like Bukowski's father."

Jennifer, who was seated directly beneath a poster of Lenin, cleared her throat. She turned our attention to Ginsberg. "I'm more interested in the poem 'America.' I think Allen Ginsberg praises Communism because he's never lived under it. He looks at it as an outsider."

"How do you look at it, as an insider?" I asked.

Jennifer looked up in the air and thought about this question. During her pause, Qing Fong jumped back in. "The problem is in the corrupt leaders, not in Communism. We should never give up our values." For a student who hadn't said a word in class all year, Qing Fong was rolling. She wasn't the only one. For the next two hours, the conversation popped. Kevin expressed skepticism. Isabel had hope. Qing Fong wanted to return to the past. Jennifer wanted to forget about it. It was Vivian, however, who ended the discussion for the day.

"All of this is very important," she told the class. "But there is something more important than poetry or any of this work." I had no idea what she was talking about, but all of the other students were grinning. Jennifer scooted out into the hall and returned with a cake that had apparently been waiting for me. The other students cheered and applauded. The cake had twenty-two lit candles, "One for each class we have had together," Isabel explained. It was chocolate frosted, and glazed with the following words: "Never forget us, Mike! Guiyang can always be your home!"

I blew out my candles, cut the cake, and took a bite. It was delicious.

◇

I left Guiyang a few days later without much ceremony. Everyone from Ah Ge to the Wang girls offered to escort me to the train station for a final farewell, but I wanted to make the journey from Gui Da to the center of town on my own. The solitude gave me time to soak in a few more Guiyang memories. I had my massive, bursting backpack strapped on, and an equally large duffel bag in tow. The doorman of the number 90 bus pulled me onboard, laughing at the amount of gear I was struggling to carry. "You must be going home," he said as I slumped into an open seat. I nodded and homesickness flooded over me. I was suddenly aching to see my mom and dad, my brother and his family, and all my friends. I had a visceral yearning to eat a bagel, watch a Phillies game, and lie in the grass and look up at a clear, blue sky.

Before I knew it, I was on a plane bound for JFK International Airport. I knew my emotions were out of whack when I started crying during the in-flight movie, *Fantastic Four: Rise of the Silver Surfer*. Mr. Fantastic's wedding vows to the Invisible Woman struck me as the most beautiful ever spoken. A few tears fell into my chicken cordon bleu. As happy as I was to be heading for the comforts and certainties of home, I already missed life in Guiyang. I looked down at my in-flight meal and yearned for one more order of pulled noodles, some twice-fried pork, or even a shot of deer cock wine. I wanted an old woman next to me, offering me a bite of chicken foot.

Kosher would never feel quite the same.

Afterword

In the summer of 2010, I returned to China. I spent June and July in Beijing teaching English to wealthy Chinese teenagers who would soon head off to boarding school in America. They came to class—held high in a gleaming office tower complete with air-conditioning and Wi-Fi—sporting iPads and Black-Berrys. I earned more each week than I had in a year as a PCV. I took the subway to work every day. I had a cup of coffee with my breakfast each morning. I saw Western movies in stadium-seating theaters rather than on pirated DVDs. My days at a rickety lectern in a soot-stained classroom adorned with pictures of Mao and Marx seemed impossibly distant.

For the first few weeks in Beijing, I felt like a country mouse. My Guizhou-eye view of life in China left me agog at the capital city's wealth and speed. I quickly acclimated to life in the Chinese fast lane, however, and got swept up in the excitement of a city exploding with vitality, money, and ambition. Most of all, I finally got a dose of China's confidence. A good, strong dose. For the first time, I was able to view China through the frame provided by American pundits. Beijing had the swagger of a young Mike Tyson; the city knew what kind of punch it packed. Guiyang, by contrast, was the skinny, acne-scarred kid in the corner. Or, as Qing Fong once put it, Guiyang is a chicken, helplessly different from China's wealthier, hawkish coastal cities. The other billion really do live a world apart.

◇

At the end of the program in Beijing, I hopped on a plane bound for Guiyang. I found the city much the same, though a lot had changed for the people. Dean Wang had finally been allowed to retire and had moved in with his son, a newly hired English professor at Gui Da. Word was the son would someday follow in his father's footsteps and become a leader at the school.

Jennifer was single again. Good Name Zhou held on to her for about a year, but she now insisted she was committed to a life as a bachelorette. "There are three types of women in China," she told me. "Those who are married, those who are going to get married, and those with high salaries. Chinese men just can't stand to date women who are more successful than they are, so I'll just have to be happy alone."

Coach Qin was back in Shanghai. Gui Da failed its inspection and did not become a "key university." There was therefore no more need for a basketball team.

Kevin graduated and moved to Shenzhen with Shitty. He found a good job as an English teacher in a private school. Rumor was they would soon get married.

◇

All this news helped me feel reconnected to my former life. After spending a night in a hotel downtown, and another night staying in the foreign-guest hostel at Gui Da, I was ready for my final bit of follow-up. I woke early on a Sunday and headed for the Wang village.

I crossed the highway, walked along the river, and meandered the still-familiar dirt paths at the foot of the Gui Mountains. I passed under the archway at the entrance to the village, glancing at new propaganda posters. My reading skills were rusty after two years outside of China and I had trouble understanding the characters. What other hard-earned knowledge would fade with time?

The propaganda had changed, but the streets were still covered in excrement, construction materials still littered the fields nearest the main road, and the houses were still dilapidated. I watched a child squat in the middle of the road for an early morning poo. It was good to be back.

I arrived at the courtyard to the Wang house shortly after 7:00 a.m. The pigsty was empty, the doorway was open, and one of the girls was pounding corn husks that had been laid on the ground to dry. The wooden tool she was using made a repetitive *thwack!* The girl had her back to me, so I couldn't tell which of the Wang girls was hard at work. Was it Big Twin? Wang Number One? Three years may as well have been thirty in the world of teenage growth spurts.

"Hello," I called out in English as the girl took a break from her work. She turned to me and dropped her tool to the ground. Her jaw fell almost as far. "Mike!" she yelled. "You have returned!" She was taller than when I had last seen her and her skin had tanned to a deep brown. She had crow's feet at the corners of her eyes—wrinkles that made her look older than her sixteen years—and a new, short haircut. The smile, however, was the same, and was unmistakably Little Twin's. Only she wasn't so little anymore: she was pregnant.

I stared at her belly. "I'm married now," she told me with a grin.

"So I gathered."

She scooped up her threshing tool and gestured for me to enter the courtyard. The Wangs were no doubt used to old friends and family dropping by without much notice—with a single cell phone as the only way to contact the family, they were largely incommunicado—and Little Twin quickly regained her composure. She looked me over head to toe. "You look too thin," she told me. "You're also losing your hair already. Other than that, you look the same." Little Twin approached me and laid a hand on my forearm. "I'm happy you have returned," she said simply.

She went back to work. "Let me finish this quickly, then I'll fix you some food." She began threshing more corn husks. "This will only take me a minute." *Thwack!* "Meanwhile, I'll tell you the news." *Thwack!* "We sold the pigs because my oldest sister will be going to graduate school. She will study in Chongqing and learn chemistry. The family is very proud." *Thwack!* "My grandmother died, and afterwards I came home. I have stopped criticizing my father. My husband and I live here now in the family home." *Thwack!* "Big Twin is still working at my uncle's restaurant." *Thwack!* "The best news is that Wang Number One did very well on the high school entrance exam. She is attending Guiyang's number-one high school." Little Twin gave the wheat a final blow and wiped a bead of sweat from her forehead. Her whirlwind summary of life during the last few years left me momentarily speechless.

"Are you happy?" I eventually asked.

She thought for a moment, her face looking very grown-up. A breeze blew from the west carrying the smells of manure and freshly cut grass. "I miss climbing trees," she responded. "If you keep on climbing them, you'll have to do it alone."

Little Twin stretched her back and patted her belly. Her life will be one of sore muscles, long days in the sun, and physical toil. Perhaps iPads await her children.

Acknowledgments

I am grateful to the people who inspired me to join the Peace Corps: Becca Cahill, Larry Van Meter, and the students and teachers at Darrow School and Moorestown Friends School.

I owe any success I found in China to the Peace Corps staff, to the faculty and students at Gui Da, and to my fellow PCVs. Special thanks to Zhu Kui, Nick, Dylan, Erin and Brian, Mary, Derek, Casey, Kelsey, and the other China 11s.

I returned home to the caring and inspiring community at St. Paul's School, in Concord, N.H. Thank you to all in Millville who helped me remember how to teach, eat, and pray in America. Thanks also to Putney Student Travel for helping me get back to China, and for introducing me to Julia.

I returned home with no idea how to write a book. Dave Sirota and Will Lippincott are my Marx and Einstein. The team at Henry Holt—from David Patterson who first believed in this project, to Gillian Blake whose patience and wisdom can be found on every page of the book—are my politburo.

I am unendingly grateful to be in the Levy family. My brother is both the funniest and smartest person I've ever met, as well as the second-best father. The gold medal goes to Dad, the kindest, most giving person I know. The Levy men, however, would be totally screwed without Mom. She is the hardest-working of us all, as well as the most selfless. I live to be the pale embodiment of these three people, all of whom have taught me how to love.

About the Author

MIKE LEVY is an educator, writer, and traveler, currently teaching at Saint Ann's School in Brooklyn, New York. Along with teaching at Guizhou University, he has served on the faculty of St. Paul's School, Moorestown Friends School, Darrow School, and Putney Student Travel.

While in the United States, Mike does his best to keep kosher. While in China, he eats anything with four legs but the table.